Not L
in t
Kinga

Roy Williamson is an Honorary Assistant Bishop in the Diocese of Southwell and was previously Bishop of Bradford (1984–91) and Bishop of Southwark (1991–98). He was also Archdeacon of Nottingham and the incumbent of three parishes in that city. His previous books include *Can You Spare a Minute* and *For Such a Time as This* (published by DLT) and *Joyful Uncertainty* and *Open Return* (both Triangle). He is married with three sons, two daughters and seven grandchildren.

At that time the disciples came to Jesus and asked, 'Who is the greatest in the kingdom of heaven?' He called a child, whom he put among them, and said, 'Truly, I tell you, unless you change and become like children, you will never enter the kingdom of heaven. Whoever becomes humble like this child is the greatest in the kingdom of heaven.'

(Matthew 18.1–4)

Not Least
in the
Kingdom

Roy Williamson

TRIANGLE

Published in Great Britain in 2001
Triangle
SPCK
Holy Trinity Church
Marylebone Road
London NW1 4DU

British Library Cataloguing-in-Publication Data

A catalogue record for this book is available from
the British Library

ISBN 0–281–05421–5

Typeset by Pioneer Associates, Perthshire
Printed in Great Britain by
Omnia Books, Glasgow

Contents

For
Anne
by no means least in the kingdom of heaven

I am grateful to my editor Alison Barr for her encouragement and helpful advice and to Jean Cherry for reading the text and offering suggestions for improvement. All biblical quotations are taken from the New Revised Standard Version.

Introduction

A few months before retirement I achieved a double first. I paid my first visit to the Albert Hall and I experienced my first BBC Promenade concert. The music in the first half was by Messiaen – an acquired taste. The second included a beautiful symphony by Bruckner – enthralling and uplifting. But it wasn't just the music that captivated me. I was fascinated by the lady in the black evening gown who sat in the back row of the orchestra. She never moved a muscle or produced an instrument until the last minute of the symphony; then, suddenly getting to her feet, she produced a small triangle, struck it four times and sat down again, her evening's work complete. The symphony ended only seconds later to thunderous applause from the audience.

The leader of the orchestra was singled out for special acclaim; with prolonged enthusiasm the audience demanded the conductor's return to the podium three times and the whole orchestra received a standing ovation – including the lady with the triangle.

Her contribution, though small, was vital. The composer had written her four notes into the score. Without them, the symphony would not have been complete.

That, in essence, is what this little book is about, and why I feel constrained to put pen to paper. It is written in praise for and appreciation of those countless people who make a vital contribution to the total life of both church and community, and without whose skill and commitment, the 'symphony' would be incomplete. They provide the support so essential to those who carry the responsibility of leadership.

Rarely is attention focused on those who play the triangle, or the second fiddle for that matter. They neither attempt nor desire to make a name for themselves. Nevertheless, in the chapters that follow, I hope that some may recognize their particular contribution to the overall harmony and impact of the symphony of life and service. If they do, I hope they will be encouraged, inspired and, in some small way, affirmed in their invaluable work for the kingdom of God.

They may feel themselves to be a million miles from people like Ananias, Barnabas, Priscilla, Aquila and the others, but I doubt if God would place such a distance between them. Most of them would be embarrassed and surprised to learn that their contribution was in any way considered significant. That is the measure of their humility and devotion.

Of course, they demand no thanks and require no reward for what they do. But those whose leadership and influence is strengthened because of their support would be lacking in love if they fail to recognize and affirm their ministry and give thanks to God for them.

The contents of this book are not a series of old sermons or Bible studies to which I have given the kiss of life, or a quick burst in the microwave, in order to serve them up to unsuspecting and indiscriminate readers. Rather, they are simple, biblically based reflections on a theme. They may help individuals in their private devotions. They could provide small groups with a focus for study and prayer. They could be used for private meditation within the silence of a 'quiet day'. In whatever circumstances they are used, I sincerely hope they will inspire gratitude for those who appear destined to play second fiddle, or the triangle, in God's orchestra. Given the true nature of the kingdom of God, such people may ultimately, and to their great astonishment, discover that, far from being insignificant instruments, they have been major players all along!

I

Ananias
who overcame fear and prejudice

It has been said that life is lived looking forward
and understood looking backward. Most of us would
testify to the truth of that statement from our own
experience. Things which appeared to be disasters
have, on reflection, turned out to be blessings, while
events initially perceived as triumphs have turned
out to be the precursors of prolonged trouble. It is
only as we look back that we can discern, with full
understanding, what God was doing in our lives, or
what selfish or unselfish motives lay behind the
decisions we took or the path we chose.

Ananias, looking back, must have seen his vision
from God and his visit to Saul of Tarsus as repre-
senting not just the highlight of his life, but, indeed,
the very purpose for which he was born. It was a truly
amazing experience for both Saul and Ananias. In
prospect, it looked terrifying; in retrospect, it was a
glorious turning point in the life of the Christian
Church.

Out of the shadows

Ananias is mentioned only twice in the Bible – in two different accounts of the same story (Acts 9 and 22). He emerges out of the shadows of relative obscurity to take part in one of the most dramatic and seminal encounters of Christian history. He comes on to the stage not as a high-profile figure but as a humble follower of Jesus Christ, who is alert to what God wants to say to him. At the mention of his name, he places himself at God's disposal – 'Here I am, Lord'. It is only when he hears what God wants him to do that his fear and prejudice come all too readily to the surface. He was taken unawares.

As a young Christian, about to begin my public ministry, I recall being encouraged by a wise and godly friend to use the following simple prayer at the beginning of each day:

> Lord, prepare me for what you have
> prepared for me, and give me wisdom
> to know your will and courage to do it.

The prayer is a good one and easily said, but the reality is not always so easily understood and accepted. I feel sure that Ananias, far from feeling prepared for the task spelt out by God in his vision, was shattered and thrown into confusion by it. This is a reaction which is not uncommon when faced with an unexpected challenge – especially if there is every possibility of 'getting it wrong' and finishing up as an embarrassing failure. Costly challenges and demands rarely present themselves at convenient moments. All too often they arrive when we are already fully occupied with pressing matters of a personal or public nature. In such circumstances, it is all too easy to misread the situation, get things out of perspective and make wrong choices.

At first glance, however, it seemed that Ananias had little choice in the matter before him. Not only did God want to send him as his messenger to the one who had been the scourge of all who named the name of Jesus, but Saul already knew that Ananias was on his way! It could be construed as moral blackmail, especially since he told Ananias what he'd done; more likely, though, it was an indication of God's trust in him.

The right person

God knew what he was doing in choosing Ananias, who, though probably unaware of it, had been prepared for this very moment.

He is described as a 'disciple' of Jesus (Acts 9.10). In other words he was a follower of the Way, the name given to the new movement that we have come to call Christianity. But he is also referred to as a 'devout man according to the law and well spoken of by all the Jews living there' (Acts 22.12). God had chosen his man well. Ananias was a highly regarded Jew living in Damascus; indeed, at the time of his conversion, Saul had been *en route* for Damascus to persecute people like him (Acts 9.2).

Saul had been devastated by his encounter on the

Damascus road with the risen Jesus. It must have been a tremendous shock for him to realize that in persecuting Christians on behalf of God, it was really God he had been persecuting! How crucial it was, therefore, following this astonishing revelation, for him to be approached by a follower of the Way who was also, like him, a devout Jew. Ananias became a living example of a very important truth: namely, that it was possible to observe both traditional Jewish values and those laid down by Christ because 'the two were not at odds with each other, they were cut from the same cloth' (Dunn, 1996). He was the right man in the right place at the right time. God had prepared him for what he had prepared for him.

Our experiences of being God's person for God's moment may not be as dramatic, or seminal for the Church, as that of Ananias, but they will have their own measure of significance and fulfilment.

This was illustrated for me one summer Sunday evening outside the church where I was minister. A Guest Service was being held and people in the locality had received special invitations. A rather quiet and diminutive lady from the congregation had volunteered to stand outside and encourage passers-by to come inside. About ten minutes before the service began, a giant of a man approached her and somewhat belligerently asked, 'Can anybody go in there?' 'Yes, of course,' she replied. 'I can't read or write,' he said, in a fairly intimidating manner. 'That's all right,' she said. 'I'll come in with you.' But she didn't just come in with him, she deliberately found him a seat beside the one person in the church whose professional skill was teaching adults to read and write.

It was the beginning of a deep and lasting friendship, and also of a new discipleship, as the erstwhile illiterate, over a period of time, was taught to read and write. He became a most valued member of that local church and community. And it all came about because of the courageous and wise witness of the one whom God had prepared for what he had prepared for her.

Fear and prejudice

The large man whom the diminutive lady met outside the church was an unknown stranger. Saul was a stranger to Ananias, but he was certainly not unknown. On the contrary, he was infamous. Wherever Christians met to worship God in those early days, they were conscious of the dark shadow of fear caused by the persecuting zeal of Saul of Tarsus. So Ananias, having opened his ear to the voice of God calling him, now opened his heart to God in response to what God was asking him to do. His forthright reaction could be interpreted as, 'You can't be serious. You're asking me to go and minister to one who has come to my home town with a warrant for my arrest in his pocket!'

We know nothing of Ananias' domestic situation. He might have had a wife and children; he certainly had friends and colleagues. And all of these might be put at risk if rumours about Saul's conversion proved false and he was still intent in destroying the disciples of Jesus. The awesome experience of receiving a vision from God must have vied uneasily with a natural fear and prejudice that most of the Church still felt regarding Saul. Ananias couldn't prevent himself spelling them out to God. 'Lord, I have heard from many about this man, how much evil he has done to your saints in Jerusalem; and here he has authority from the chief priests to bind all who invoke your name' (Acts 9.13–14).

It was a natural reaction and all the better for being openly expressed, for it resulted in God explaining his great purpose for Saul and, indeed, for the Church which Paul had been persecuting. 'Go, for he is an instrument whom I have chosen to bring my name before Gentiles and kings and before the people of Israel; I myself will show him how much he must suffer for the sake of my name' (Acts 9.15–16).

Chosen and obedient

I believe it was at this point that Ananias began to get things into perspective. A citizen of Damascus, he had been asked by God to 'get up and go' a relatively short distance to the street called Straight, where Saul was praying and waiting. But Saul was about to be commissioned by God to travel a much greater distance, both in theological and geographical terms. He would be required to cross religious barriers and national boundaries in order to spread the gospel he had tried to destroy. He was to be a witness to all the world of the power of the living Christ.

Saul was God's chosen instrument, destined to be

the great missionary to the Gentiles. Ananias was also a chosen instrument, sent by God to a man whose world had been turned upside down. Morally crushed, physically blinded and in desperate need of help, Saul waited in hope for the coming of Ananias. Later, when describing his experience of the risen Christ on the Damascus road, and his subsequent call to preach the gospel, Saul, renamed Paul, could say, 'I was not disobedient to the heavenly vision' (Acts 26.19). Ananias could say exactly the same thing, because in essence the content of God's vision to him was a call to obedience. Twice during the course of that vision he received the instruction to 'get up and go' to minister to Paul. The Church is forever grateful that he was not disobedient to that heavenly vision. And I can't resist a smile when I read that, after he had laid his hands on Saul and delivered God's message as instructed, this humble, rather timid disciple had the temerity to tell Saul to get up and go: 'And now why do you delay? Get up, be baptized, and have your sins washed away, calling on his name' (Acts 22.16).

God's trust in the obedience of his servant Ananias was not misplaced. Despite his initial fear and prejudice, he had done exactly what he had been asked to do – well, almost! Actually, he added something of his own. He had the sensitivity to recognize the conflicting emotions that must have been raging in the mind and heart of Saul, following his traumatic experience on the Damascus road. His foundations had been shaken, his zeal had been misdirected, his past lay in tatters and his future was uncertain. He was lonely, blind and fearful. So Ananias, before he delivers the message God had given him, lays his hands on the head of Saul and calls him 'Brother Saul'. With the laying on of hands, Saul receives his sight. But in the use of that word 'Brother', I believe he was receiving something else, namely a deep and practical reassurance of love and forgiveness. Following his conversion, it was the first word he had heard from the lips of those he had been persecuting. In sending Ananias, God had indeed chosen the right man, one who was not only obedient but who also put flesh on the message he had been given to deliver.

Nothing more is heard of Ananias. His departure from the stage is as sudden as his appearance on it. But the story of Paul and his massive contribution to the life of the Church and the spread of the gospel would have been incomplete without this faithful, sensitive and obedient disciple of Jesus.

2

Andrew
who kept things moving

Standing at the church door to greet people as they leave after a service can be a delightful or demoralizing experience. Some smile sweetly and say, 'Lovely service, vicar' – even if they've been bored to tears! A few will be ready to do battle about the length of the sermon or the noise from the children, while others will whisper a quiet 'thank you' for some blessing received. But there's always someone who will insist on claiming the undivided attention of the minister, often about something inconsequential, thus preventing him or her from having any meaningful contact with others leaving the church. Great pastoral and diplomatic skill is needed to help that person move on, without causing offence.

No such skill was needed for Albert, however. He always hung back until almost everyone else had gone, and then, with a shy smile, would hand me a postcard with some names on it and say, 'Vicar, I've noticed these people have been missing from the congregation for the past two or three weeks. Would

you like me to call and see if they are all right?' Often
the postcard would also make me aware of those who
were sick or in hospital and needed visiting.

Some might have found Albert's attitude intrusive,
but I wasn't one of them. I thanked God for him and
the profound effect he had upon my ministry of pastoral care to a large congregation. He noticed things
that I and others had missed. He never complained
about things I hadn't done but gently and unobtru-
sively provided me with a pastoral *aide-mémoire*.
Often I received credit for being so alert to the needs
of others, but much of it was due to the pastoral sensitivity of Albert. He was not interested in finding
fault, nor was he looking for 'Brownie points' from
the vicar, but he shared my compassionate concern
for people, and was deeply committed to moving
matters on for the sake of the kingdom of God.

Though doubtless unaware of it, Albert had
acquired something of the spirit of Andrew, one of
the first disciples of Jesus.

A kindred spirit

Not much is known about Andrew, but the little that
we do know marks him out as a person who was
eager to keep things moving for the sake of the
kingdom.

He lived in the long shadow of his more illustrious
brother, Simon; indeed, when people spoke of
Andrew, they described and identified him in relation to his brother – 'Andrew, Simon Peter's brother'
(John 1.40). Clearly, Andrew was not as well known

as his brother. It says much for his strength of character, however, that he never revealed a trace of resentment at having to play second fiddle to Simon Peter. This is all the more remarkable since he, along with Simon, were the first disciples to be called by Jesus (Mark 1.16). And given the circumstances of that call, it is typical of the man that he remained free from bitterness when he was not included among Jesus' special group of friends. He, along with Simon, and the brothers James and John, were the first four disciples called by Jesus – they left all and followed him. But on those seminal occasions, on the Mount of Transfiguration and in the Garden of Gethsemane, for instance, it was Peter, James and John who were invited to accompany Jesus. Andrew was excluded from the inner circle (Mark 9.2; 14.32–33).

We might all too easily dismiss this as of little consequence, but my pastoral experience, both as a minister and as a leader in the church, leaves me with the conviction that it would be foolish to do so. The desire for recognition and reward is not absent from followers of Jesus Christ. James and John, for instance, were hoping for privileged places in the kingdom (Matthew 20.20–28), while Peter was never backward about coming forward. As spokesman for all the disciples, he said to Jesus, with reference to the coming kingdom, 'Look, we have left everything and followed you. What then will we have?' (Matthew 19.27).

On the surface, that is not too far removed from the common sentiment expressed by many today when faced with a new challenge, namely, 'What's in it for me?!' And when it comes to appointments, both within the leadership of the national Church or, indeed, within the congregation of the local church, 'Why him (or her) and not me?' is a question often asked and rarely answered satisfactorily. It seems, however, that Andrew already knew and was totally satisfied with the answer – so he didn't even bother to ask the question. To him it was obvious that Peter was the proper person to be at the right hand of Jesus and to become leader of the apostles. So, as John's record makes clear (John 1.35–42), Andrew became the facilitator of that purpose. He helped to move things on by bringing his brother to Jesus.

A captivating vision

It all began, writes John, in the Transjordan, where John the Baptist was preaching and bearing witness to the coming Jesus. Suddenly and dramatically, he points to Jesus walking by and says, 'Look, here is the Lamb of God!' I can imagine every eye in the crowd being fastened on Jesus. Andrew was no exception. But he, and an unnamed disciple, did something more. They followed Jesus in the way. He was not prepared to let opportunities pass, but was committed to keep things moving. So he responded to the witness of the Baptist and followed his heart by walking after Jesus.

There is no historical compatibility between the detail of John's account and those recorded in Matthew and Mark. John, writing later than the others, wanted to emphasize certain fundamental truths about discipleship and, as he spells them out, Andrew, with his desire to move things on, is central to his purpose.

As Andrew, and the other disciple, follow in the way, Jesus turns and confronts them with a challenge: 'What are you looking for?' he asks. Significantly, these are the first words Jesus speaks in the Gospel of John. They form a simple question, but deep within lies the challenge to all would-be disciples. Are you looking for a hero, a teacher, a guru? Are you wanting someone to cling to, someone to make you famous? Or are you looking for your deepest self and the most profound truths about life? Are you searching for reality? 'What are you looking for?' is a question put to everyone, and at some point we all must answer it.

The two disciples answer Jesus' question with another question: 'Rabbi (Teacher), where are you staying?' At this point, the question is nothing more than a request for his local address. But, as always in John's Gospel, we are conscious of a deeper layer of meaning emerging from the theme of 'abiding' (see Chapters 14 and 15). The place where Jesus 'abides' is the goal of the human journey, for Jesus 'abides' in the Father. As Andrew and the others are later to discover, the going to abide with Jesus is a foreshadowing of the truth that they would one day abide in Jesus as Jesus abides in the Father.

It seems, therefore, that Andrew's question is not just a request for information about our Lord's local B and B, but is a deep-seated, perhaps unconscious, desire to know the source of Jesus' inspiration, power and authority, to discover to whom he is bonded.

Immediately, they receive an open invitation. 'Come and see', says Jesus. So they go to stay with him – and life is never to be the same again. We don't know what transpired during their time together, but we do know that they were captivated by what they saw and heard and discovered. They moved on in their awareness of who Jesus was. They had followed one whom the Baptist had declared to be 'the Lamb of God' and one whom they believed was a holy teacher. But time spent in his presence convinced them that they had found the Messiah, God's anointed One.

In these few verses John outlines a pattern, which he later develops, of discipleship, in terms of respond-ing to testimony about Jesus, following him on the way, searching for truth, and making the life-changing discovery of who he is, followed by the sharing of that good news with others. In all this the initiative lies with Jesus, but he found in Andrew a person eager to respond and keep things moving on.

Bringing others to Jesus

It was this desire to keep things moving for the sake of the kingdom that produced Andrew's best known characteristic, namely that of bringing people to Jesus. Here, his immediate action on leaving the house where he had spent such quality time with Jesus was to find his brother and bring him to Jesus (John 1.41–42). 'He first found his brother Simon, and said to him, "We have found the Messiah".'

Perhaps as Jesus had talked with Andrew and the other disciple during their stay with him, the immensity of the task which he hoped to perform began to dawn on them. Captivated by the vision,

Andrew felt not only the need to share it with his brother, but also that his brother had the kind of personality and energy to make a major contribution to its realization. It was a conviction shared by Jesus, for when Andrew brought Simon, Jesus renamed him Cephas (translated Peter), meaning rock. It was an indication that Jesus had plans for Peter and that he would perform a key function in the foundation and development of his Church. Andrew's unselfish attitude results in him bringing to Jesus the one who is to become 'the Rock' – the solid character on whom he will build the foundations of his Church.

A borrowed picnic

But this passion of Andrew's for bringing people to Jesus was demonstrated at another formative moment in the ministry of Jesus and his training of the early disciples. The feeding of the five thousand, with its massive underlying symbolism, including the portrayal of Jesus as the Bread of Life, was a classic example of Andrew's eagerness to keep things moving for the sake of the kingdom (John 6.1–15).

The popularity of Jesus was on the increase. His teaching was on the wavelength of ordinary people and his love for them was evident; small wonder that he attracted large crowds.

Amazingly, his obvious concern for needy individuals was matched by his practical compassion for the multitude. There was a wholeness about his ministry. He was anxious about their physical as well as their spiritual needs. Man may not live by bread alone, but he can't live without it. After following Jesus up the mountainside, the multitude was hungry and Jesus was aware of it. He took the initiative and tested Philip, one of his disciples, with the problem. 'Where are we to buy bread for these people to eat?' Philip, bless him, got bogged down with the financial implications of the challenge, and said, 'Six months' wages would not buy enough bread for these people to eat.' Jesus saw the multitude as sheep without a shepherd and longed to feed them. Philip saw the multitude as an administrative problem.

It was at that point that Andrew, wanting to move things on, brought a young lad to Jesus and said, 'There is a boy here who has five barley loaves and two fish.' On the surface it seemed a silly intervention, and Andrew realized it, for he added, 'But what are they among so many people?' Philip knew that human resources were inadequate. So did Andrew, but he wasn't prepared to leave it there. He offered the contents of a borrowed picnic basket to Jesus. It seemed pathetically absurd as a resource, but it was something for Jesus to work with, and in his hands it proved more than adequate. Human resources, however small, when placed at the disposal of God can achieve unimaginable results. Little is always much in the hands of Christ.

Andrew has been an inspiration to Christians in every age and since the eighth century has been regarded as the patron saint of Scotland. In the church calendar, his feast day is 30 November, when the Anglican Communion, motivated by his example of bringing others to Jesus, widely observes St

Andrewstide as a special period of intercession for missionary work.

For me, Andrew is the epitome of all those of a positive spirit in every local church and community of faith, who, though circumstances require them to play second fiddle, do so with skill, sensitivity and enthusiasm. Thus they keep things moving for the sake of the kingdom and help realize the vision of God's glory and purpose.

3

Barnabas
who built bridges of understanding

On the day in 1978 when I became Archdeacon of Nottingham, I had another surprise. I found myself to be the possessor of a special seal, that went with the job and was stamped on every legal document I issued. It consisted of an embossed engraving of an open hand with an open eye in the palm.

I am still not entirely sure what the symbol on the seal actually meant, though the suggestion that an archdeacon acts as the eye of the bishop seemed plausible, if slightly uncomplimentary. So I lived in the expectation that one day some knowledgeable person would inform me that it was the symbol of the Ancient Order of Leprechauns, or something equally mysterious.

However, I had my own explanation. To me, it symbolized the balanced nature of my new work. It spoke of the need for vision and pastoral care, an open eye to see opportunity or need and an open hand to offer practical help and support.

It is a symbol that always comes to mind when I

read of the ministry of Barnabas, the companion of
Paul. The latter became the more famous, but without a doubt Barnabas is one of the most attractive
figures in the early Church, and his contribution to
its mission was considerable. It is not without significance that the first time we see this wealthy Levite
from Cyprus he is offering practical help and support
to those in need (Acts 4.36–37). The warm testimony
given to him – 'He was a good man, full of the Holy
Spirit and of faith' (Acts 11.24) – marks him out as a
person of rare quality. It also gives the clue to his
ability as a builder of bridges of understanding.

Making connections

It was a former Bishop of Winchester, John V. Taylor,
who famously described the Holy Spirit as the 'go-
between God'. He is the one who makes connections
between people and across the ages, the creative
Spirit who links people with God and each other, and
who brings God's past action and future glory into
our present experience. As Bishop Taylor wrote, 'My
own attempts to understand the Holy Spirit has
convinced me that he is active in those experiences
that are very common – experiences of recognition,
sudden insight, an influx of awareness when you
wake up and become alive to something . . . Every
time a human being cries, "Ah! I see it now!" that's
what I mean by the Holy Spirit' (Taylor, 1972).

The fullness of the Holy Spirit within Barnabas
seems to have equipped him for his special ministry
of making connections and building bridges between

people and churches. He was, literally, a Godsend to Paul. Without him, Paul's widespread missionary endeavour might never have got off the ground, for the Christians in Jerusalem appeared to be a dubious bunch.

Though there seems to be some confusion surrounding Paul's immediate work after his encounter with Ananias (Acts 9.10–25; see also Galatians 1.18–20), the Christians in Jerusalem were rather sceptical of his conversion. The early chapters of Acts include some quite remarkable things done by the apostles in the name of Christ. Their zeal was great, their faith was strong: 'And day by day the Lord added to their number those who were being saved.' Yet, strangely, they seemed to draw the line at Paul! Paul was, as it were, a bridge too far. When he came to Jerusalem and wanted to join them, their faith was overwhelmed by their fear of his reputation as an enemy of the church – 'They did not believe that he was a disciple.' There seemed to be something of a stand-off.

Barnabas came to the rescue. He met with Paul and brought him to the Jerusalem apostles, describing to them not only Paul's encounter with the risen Christ on the Damascus road, but also his conversion and subsequently courageous preaching of the gospel in Damascus. Thanks to the advocacy of Barnabas, they were won over, for they accepted Paul on his recommendation. Filled with the Holy Spirit, he had made the necessary, and far-reaching, connection between Paul and the Jerusalem church. Paul had been drawn into the company of the apostles – an important milestone in his life and also in the life of the Church of Jesus Christ.

Bridge-building

It is one of the ways of God that when his disciples prove faithful over one task, he tends to reward them by giving them even more responsibility. So it was with Barnabas. As the Church began to grow in numbers and extend geographically, it faced new challenges and opportunities. The need for bridge-building increased. Barnabas was the man for the task. Paul was to be placed at the forefront of God's mission strategy, but its success would owe much to the encouragement and practical skill of his companion. This was particularly true as the Church began to cross Gentile frontiers.

Despite the compulsion of the Holy Spirit given at Pentecost, the church in Jerusalem had not been all that energetic in moving outwards. But the persecution following the martyrdom of Stephen changed all that (Acts 11.19–30), and members of the Jerusalem church were scattered as far as Antioch. Initially they preached to the Jews in that city, but some of them began to spread the good news of Jesus among the Gentiles. Their preaching met with success, for 'a great number became believers and turned to the Lord'.

The church in Jerusalem, having previously been suspicious of Paul (Acts 9.26), and more latterly critical of Peter for mixing with Gentiles (Acts 11.3), on this occasion revealed a more generous spirit. They did the right thing and sent the right man, Barnabas, as their representative to investigate the events in Antioch. It was a wise decision. Barnabas had a large heart and proven skills in personal relations.

It wasn't a matter of human cleverness or sweet-talking. He was a genuine, generous and godly man. He recognized the grace of God at work among them and rejoiced. He couldn't claim any personal credit for what was taking place; he was just glad that God was at work among them, and he encouraged them all to keep the faith.

But he did more. He helped the new young church to get established. He did this not only by his own pastoral work but also by his wise assessment of their future needs. He didn't selfishly or foolishly try to 'go it alone'. He knew his own limitations. He knew that the developments at Antioch were a significant breakthrough for the gospel in that whole region of Syria. He also knew the ideal person to ensure that the young church kept on the right lines. His name was Paul.

Partners in mission

Barnabas went to Tarsus, and having found Paul brought him to Antioch. Once again he was making connections and building bridges – with deep understanding. A man of vision, he was aware of Paul's value to the mission of God, so he drew him back, as it were, into the mainstream of the church's outward movement. The fact that Paul was a Jew with Gentile sympathies was a distinct advantage in that situation.

Paul's courage, theological competence, and powerful advocacy for the faith would also be sources of strength and comfort to this young church as it came under criticism from Jewish and Gentile opponents.

So for a whole year Barnabas and Paul worked together in leadership. Their influence was deep and widespread, for 'they taught a great many people, and it was at Antioch that the disciples were first called Christians'. It was a name coined by the Roman authorities. They clearly observed that the followers of this new religious movement in their midst were characterized by a belief in Jesus Christ and by lives lived in his name. What apparently began as a nickname, 'the Christ-ones', stuck.

Nickname or not, it was an indication that a young church was growing in strength and confidence, so much so that the motivation to cross the frontiers of mission into the surrounding regions became irresistible, as God made his plans known to them. 'While they were worshipping the Lord and fasting, the Holy Spirit said, "Set apart for me Barnabas and Saul for the work to which I have called them." Then, after fasting and praying, they laid their hands on them and sent them out' (Acts 13.2–3). Thus began the first significant penetration of the gospel into the Gentile world, what has become known as Paul's first missionary journey.

That description is revealing, not least regarding the character of Barnabas. He was the initial leader of the mission team, but, as the tour progressed, Paul assumed that role (Acts 13.13). There was no complaint from Barnabas. He was prepared to take second place for the sake of the success of God's mission. And success it was, for though there were times of opposition and rejection, these were matched by many people coming to faith and many churches being founded. So, having by the grace of God completed their task, they returned to Antioch, where they had been commissioned. 'When they arrived, they called the church together and related all that God had done with them, and how he had opened a door of faith for the Gentiles' (Acts 14.26–27). The mission partnership between Barnabas and Paul had opened a door and built a bridge into the Gentile world.

Partners in controversy

However, mission is not without cost. Fulfilling the commission to make disciples and carry the gospel to the ends of the world produced new challenges and led to the Church's first major crisis. If it hadn't been handled wisely, this crisis could have produced a division within the Church which might never have been healed.

Barnabas and Paul were part of the problem – and they became part of the solution. That first missionary journey had resulted in Gentiles being converted to Christ. But news that Paul and Barnabas had not required their converts to be circumcised had reached the church in Jerusalem and caused an upset. The more legalistic in that church were quite put out! Given their Jewish heritage, they viewed the need for circumcision as non-negotiable. Gentiles, however, with their Hellenistic background, were averse to such a suggestion, and saw circumcision as non-essential to salvation in Christ.

It was a classic encounter between tradition on the one hand and relevance on the other. In every age, including our own, that conflict threatens to divide the Church, and in every age it calls for cool heads, generous hearts and a clear understanding of the essentials of the gospel. Barnabas had all three. Peter, Paul and James may have played a major part in the resolution of the conflict, but Barnabas' own contribution was not insignificant. His gift of building bridges of understanding was clearly in evidence as the crisis was addressed.

When some of the hard-liners from Jerusalem came to the church in Antioch and taught the need of circumcision for salvation, Paul and Barnabas engaged them in debate and questioned the relevance of such teaching for Gentile converts. It was potentially such a divisive issue that they, together with other church leaders, were sent to Jerusalem to discuss the matter with the apostles and the elders, at what has become known as the Church's first General Council (Acts 15).

It was not a wasted journey, for the assembly in Jerusalem kept silence and listened attentively to their testimony, 'as they told of all the signs and wonders that God had done through them among the Gentiles' (Acts 15.12). Their words, together with the powerful intervention of Peter and the superb summing up and decisiveness of James, helped resolve the issue. Circumcision was no longer to be considered essential. 'I have reached the decision,' said James, 'that we should not trouble those Gentiles who are turning to God.' As a further sign of their good faith, they sent representatives of the Jerusalem church to return with Barnabas and Paul to Antioch in order to reassure the church in that city. The Christians at Antioch rejoiced at the news, and were strengthened and encouraged by the ministry of their Jerusalem brothers.

Partners in conflict

Barnabas and Paul recognized that a bridge had been built that would safeguard the future of Christianity. A movement that began as Jewish had now embraced and accepted Gentiles as full members. With confidence, therefore, they settled once more into the church at Antioch, where, 'with many others, they taught and proclaimed the word of the Lord' (Acts 16.35). It sounds like an idyllic scene but, sadly, it didn't last. Division suddenly replaced unity. Harmony gave way to contention, focused on John Mark, cousin of Barnabas.

Paul, now clearly the leader of the Gentile mission, was eager to push on with the spread of the gospel. He suggested to Barnabas that they visit the converts and churches they had met on their first tour, to see how they were getting on. Barnabas was keen and wanted to take Mark with them. Paul considered Mark unreliable and didn't want him on the team. There was no bridge-building from Barnabas this time. The disagreement between him and Paul was sharp and their parting acrimonious. Barnabas took

Mark and went to Cyprus. Paul took Silas and went through Syria. An effective partnership was broken.

Was there more to the row than the person of Mark? Did they each have a hidden agenda? Was Barnabas not entirely happy with the strategy that Paul had planned or the route he wished to take? As far as Barnabas was concerned, was blood thicker than water? Did Paul feel that Mark would be a liability? It would be wrong to speculate, though it is strange that a conciliatory person like Barnabas was unable to work out a compromise. Perhaps it reveals, as Professor James Dunn says, 'how impossible it is to separate human temperament from heartfelt commitment' (Dunn, 1996).

It may seem rather odd, but I find their disagreement reassuring and encouraging, for I have always had mixed feelings about the great saints of the Church. They inspire me on the one hand and cause me to despair on the other. All too often they are described in such glowing terms as to place them, as it were, on another plane, if not another planet. They are so good, gifted and godly that ordinary mortals can never hope to emulate them.

Of course, I know it's not quite like that, but it does offer just a little encouragement to the rest of us, when occasionally they are revealed as having one toe, if not two feet, of clay. I find Barnabas all the more inspiring because of his disagreement with Paul. That incident doesn't detract one iota from the description of him as 'a good man, full of the Holy Spirit and of Faith'. Indeed, it adds lustre to the true meaning of his name, 'son of encouragement' (Acts 4.36).

Anyone with his ability, called to be a leader but prepared to become a number two in the team for the sake of the gospel, is worthy to be called a saint. The Church of God today does well to honour his name and give thanks for his life. At the same time, it needs the vision to recognize, and the courage to support, all those in both church and society who are called to the task of building bridges of understanding.

4

Matthias
who was chosen as twelfth man

As a stipendiary Reader in the Church of England in the late 1950s, I was appointed as minister-in-charge of an inner-city London church dedicated to St Matthias. On my first Sunday, there were nine people in the congregation in a building that seated five hundred. Ironically, the opening hymn was 'Christian, dost thou see them'. I could hardly sing for laughing, for it was quite difficult to see them. In true Anglican fashion, most of them were in the back row.

To be a minister in that church was a rather tough but immensely rewarding experience, though to be honest my greatest trial was having to suffer the constant reminder from my friends that 'the lot fell on Matthias' (Acts 1.26).

It was usually said with a touch of humour and a degree of reality, for circumstances often determined that St Matthias' Church had more than its fair share of trouble heaped upon it. Nevertheless, many came to faith in that place and some went on to be leaders in God's Church. For young and old, it was a place of encounter with the living God, where the experience of worship on Sunday shaped their lives and priorities for the rest of the week.

Several years later the building became redundant, and was eventually replaced by a supermarket. The Church of St Matthias had come and gone with hardly a mention in the local story of faith. Perhaps it had been particularly aptly named, for it bore one striking similarity to its patron saint – it came and went fairly quickly, and without much fuss.

Chosen to fill a gap

Little is known of Matthias other than his being chosen as twelfth man to fill the gap among the disciples caused by the untimely death of Judas. He comes and goes in the space of four verses (Acts 1.23–26). Theologians argue as to the wisdom, even the validity, of his appointment, and some write him off as of no consequence. I am not one of them. On the contrary, I have a great deal of respect for Matthias and draw inspiration and encouragement from his brief appearance in the Christian story.

The eleven disciples, recalling their own record of desertion and denial in the shadow of the cross, may have understood Judas' betrayal of Jesus, but what really must have shaken them to the core was his despairing act of suicide. Such a death was all the more poignant in the light of Christ's resurrection. It has been said that 'Judas' terminal sin was not his treachery, but his inability to believe in the possibility of forgiveness' (Alison, 1993). The other disciples, despite their own moral failure before the cross, had experienced the unconditional forgiveness of the crucified and risen Christ. Each time they met together and saw the empty chair, did they find themselves thinking, 'if only Judas had waited'? Perhaps there was a feeling of guilt that he had gone in such terrible circumstances while they, despite their failure, were rejoicing in a new start.

Was it, perhaps, this feeling of guilt that prompted Peter and the others to think about another twelfth man to occupy the chair and take the place of Judas? That may have been an unacknowledged part of their subconscious reasoning, but there seemed to be a more profound motive for making up the numbers, and they found scriptural justification for doing so (Acts 1.15–20).

Pre-empting the Spirit?

Not everyone agrees that the disciples' reason for appointing Matthias was justified. Some claim that it marked a failure of nerve in the ten days between the departure of Jesus at the Ascension and the coming of the Spirit at Pentecost. They insist that the disciples should have waited for the promised Holy Spirit, who would guide them into all truth, rather than rush into an appointment of a successor for Judas, especially since they resorted to an Old Testament method of discerning the will of God, casting lots. This equivalent of 'tossing a coin' seems rather undignified. The fact that we hear nothing more of either of the two candidates is considered by some to be an indication that the disciples pre-empted the Spirit, and got both the method and the choice wrong.

In a strange, perhaps perverse, way, the uncertainty surrounding the appointment of Matthias endears him all the more to me.

It was a difficult in-between period for the eleven apostles and the other disciples of Jesus. Did waiting for the promised Holy Spirit imply complete inactivity and a suspension of their own thought patterns and judgement? Jesus had chosen twelve apostles; one had died by his own hand, so was it not right that they should look to their Lord for a replacement?

They were clear about the qualifications needed for an apostle. He had to have followed Jesus continually from the baptism of John until the Ascension, and to have been a witness of Jesus' resurrection. The emphasis is on continuity. And I believe that the issue of continuity was one of the reasons why Luke recorded this incident, including the horror of Judas' death, in such detail. Many feel that the original choice of twelve was symbolic and concerned with continuity. Jesus had in mind the twelve tribes of Israel, and therefore chose a group of companions who would represent the true Israel. Bringing the number of apostles once more up to twelve therefore reaffirmed the continuity between the church that was about to emerge and the old Israel. There was a seamless robe between the old and the new.

Your choice, Lord

The assembled company of believers, numbering

about one hundred and twenty, seemed unanimous in their conviction that two people, Joseph and Matthias, stood out as having the necessary qualifications. So they prayed, acknowledging that only God knew the hearts of people, and asked him to make his will known through the traditional method of casting lots. It was a clear indication that they felt that they were acting neither unbelievingly nor unilaterally. Jesus had gone and the Spirit had not yet come, but God was still in charge! They saw Matthias as God's choice. 'The lot fell on Matthias; and he was added to the eleven apostles' (Acts 1.26).

It marked the beginning and the end of the recorded story of Matthias, though some traditions refer to him preaching the gospel in Ethiopia and dying in Jerusalem. Such a momentary mention in the Christian story, before disappearing into obscurity, may confirm the opinion of some that he was the wrong man in the wrong place at the wrong time! Indeed, some have strongly expressed the view that in pre-empting the Spirit's choice the assembly of believers, under Peter's leadership, forced Matthias to usurp God's ultimate choice of Paul to be twelfth man.

Silence may be golden

We may never know the whole truth, though it will be interesting to see who is named as twelfth man on the walls of the heavenly Jerusalem: 'And the wall of the city has twelve foundations and on them are the names of the twelve apostles of the Lamb' (Revelation 21.14).

However, I am uneasy about equating silence with failure or obscurity with nonentity. Even if the eleven apostles and the assembly of believers got it wrong, I am unhappy about dismissing Matthias to a waste basket labelled 'mistakes'. That would be unfair and unwise. Most of us have had to live not only with our own mistakes, but also with the mistakes of others. Often that has resulted in a refining of our character leading to a more effective life or ministry.

I have little doubt that that was also true of Matthias. The qualities which caused others to short-list him and, apparently, God to choose him as twelfth man, didn't suddenly disappear. He had much to offer and clearly was willing to place himself at the disposal of God and his Church. How God and the Church used him after that was not really his concern. It was enough that he said 'Yes' to a call that he believed came from God.

Most, if not all, of those called to leadership in the Church have gone through experiences of feeling 'out of place'. There are times when our expectations of how God might use us have proved to be very far removed from reality. There are other occasions when we are so uncertain about what God wants us to do that, like Matthias, we can only respond in obedience and faith to what the Church is asking us to do. But it is the ability to keep going and remain faithful in such circumstances that often confirms that God has indeed called us.

There is a belief in some quarters of the Church today that success is a sure sign of being in the will of God, the corollary being that failure is an indication of being out of step with God. Oh dear! How readily do we fall into the temptation of declaring what God is doing in the lives of others! Must we interpret the silence surrounding the ministry of Matthias after his appointment as an infallible indication that God had gently put him out to grass? That may or may not be the case, though it is just worth noting that there were others, like Matthew, James, son of Alphaeus, Simon the Zealot, and Judas, the son of James, mentioned in Acts 1.13, about whom Luke says nothing more.

Spin-doctors, publicists and press officers are not only found in today's media-conscious secular society; they are also found in the church. Silence is no longer seen as a virtue, and at times there seems an indecent haste to be heard saying or seen doing something that is eye-catching and media-worthy. All too often we appear to rush into print to justify our existence. Column inches or film footage are deemed as measures of success, or failure, depending on their content.

It may be that Matthias, and the circumstances surrounding his choice as twelfth man, provides those unduly concerned with attention-seeking in the Church with a reminder that God may choose to work in silence and obscurity as well as in publicity and activity. Perhaps, as an activist, that is a lesson I also must learn, for I believe that it was Ignatius of Antioch who said that a bishop was most like God when he was silent.

5

⁊⁊

Mark
who came back from failure

No one likes to be a failure. Yet, in a competitive society like ours, it has become almost an occupational hazard. Indeed, if we gave heed to the portrayal of the good life as seen through the eyes of the television advert, most of us would fall far short of that so-called standard of success.

John Mark, the cousin of Barnabas and author of the Gospel that bears his name, was considered by Paul to be a failure. This young disciple from Jerusalem had set out with Barnabas and Paul on their first missionary tour, but when they reached Perga in Pamphylia he decided to go back home. We are not told why, though Paul later referred to his departure as desertion and failure to accompany them in the work (Acts 15.37f). Was Mark unprepared for the rigours and challenges of such a journey? Was he disappointed that Paul had taken over the leadership from his cousin half-way through the tour? Was he just plain homesick? We don't know.

So, perhaps, like the scriptures, we should maintain

a discreet silence and draw a quiet veil over the event. Certainly it would be wrong to draw conclusions or construct doctrine from either silence or speculation. But, in the light of his return home and Paul's somewhat scathing description of it, we can't suspend our imagination as to the feelings of John Mark at his apparent failure, especially in view of Barnabas' later defence of him in the face of Paul (Acts 15.39). We shouldn't ignore what this sense of failure might have meant to Mark at a formative period of his life – especially if we have experienced failure ourselves.

A human disciple

There are indications that John Mark came from a well-to-do family of Christian Jews living in Jerusalem (Acts 12.12). His home was obviously a fairly substantial one, large enough to accommodate a meeting of the local congregation of believers. This was the assembly from which Mark went out to be a part of the mission team that travelled with Barnabas and Paul. It was also the congregation to which he returned – rather earlier than expected – and with a cloud hanging over him. It doesn't take too vivid an imagination to reflect on the reactions that may have surrounded his return.

I remember the occasion when my wife, Anne, and I first felt called to full-time missionary work in a difficult and lonely area of ministry in Southern Ireland. Some friends regarded it as a great step of faith. Others saw it as an act of sheer folly. Many were cautious and decided to watch and pray! By the grace of God and the help of friends, despite the most trying circumstances, we hung in there for two years before returning home to prepare for a new missionary challenge in London. It proved to be the hardest yet most formative period of our lives and in retrospect was an ideal preparation for our future ministry.

But when we returned home from Southern Ireland, some of our friends were very cool towards us. Others said, 'We told you so.' A few were openly critical and one, who should have known better, abused the privilege of the pulpit to make a scathing attack upon us by using the following passage as a pretext: 'No one who puts a hand to the plough and looks back is fit for the kingdom of God' (Luke 9.62).

So, human nature being what it is, I doubt that John Mark's return to his own local church in Jerusalem passed without comment. His commitment to go with Barnabas and Paul would have been admired and greeted with enthusiasm, at least by some. How, then, did they react to his premature homecoming? Mark was human. We can imagine, therefore, his embarrassment at the next meeting of the congregation. What explanation did he give for his early return? How did he tell them without appearing to be disloyal either to Paul or the gospel? And what about Paul's charge of desertion and lack of commitment? How did Mark handle that, within himself and among his friends? How shaken was his confidence in himself and in God?

These are the types of questions anyone possessed with normal human feelings has to grapple with when they fail, or are perceived to have failed, within either the Church or society.

Moving on from failure

However, it is not always what happens to us that determines our future, but how we react to what happens to us. Whatever shape failure takes, or whatever gloss is placed upon it, it is often accompanied by emotional and psychological baggage. Ask all those who, for instance, having offered themselves with passion and commitment for the ministry of God's Church, fail to be recommended. Some take it in their stride and most, in time, come to see the hand of God in it. Others, however, feel a deep sense of hurt and rejection, and find it hard to think of it in terms other than failure.

It is possible to dismiss such hurt out of hand as a lack of maturity, but that can be a cruel and foolish assessment, leaving the problem unresolved. Feelings of failure and rejection, whether perceived or real, need sympathetic understanding and sensitive care. Self-confidence needs to be restored, and often one's sense of worth needs to be repaired.

Mark was fortunate to have cousin Barnabas, one of the most outstanding characters of the early Church, as a model and mentor. 'Encouragement' was his middle name, and soon he is sponsoring Mark for another missionary tour. So strongly did he feel that Mark was ready for such a renewal of commitment that he stood out against Paul's refusal to have Mark on the team. It wasn't just a gentle difference of opinion. It was an angry disagreement. Barnabas wanted Mark on the team and wouldn't go without him. Paul was adamant that he wouldn't have him. So Paul and Barnabas went their separate ways (Acts 15.36–41), and, as far as we know, there is no record of them ever working together again, though there is evidence of reconciliation (1 Corinthians 9.6; Colossians 4.10).

But, with the help of Barnabas, Mark had moved on from failure. Once more he was engaged in obeying the command of Christ to spread the gospel. It was the first step on his way back, though he had to bear the weight of being the cause of the disagreement between Paul and Barnabas. It can't have been an easy load to carry, and for years, it seems, he disappeared from view.

But, whatever transpired in the intervening years, God had pleasant surprises in store for both Mark and Paul. The small step back from failure that Barnabas had encouraged and facilitated had become a giant leap forward, as Mark is seen to be an associate of Paul in the work of the gospel.

Reputation restored

What a turnaround! The breach has been repaired. No longer is there 'distance' or disagreement between Mark and Paul. The latter is in prison and Mark is with him. Paul finds him a comfort and commends him warmly to others, asking them to treat him properly! (Colossians 4.10). Paul's letter to Philemon, also written from prison, goes even further and refers to Mark as his fellow-worker (Philemon 24). But perhaps most poignant of all is Paul's plea to the young Timothy (2 Timothy 4.11). Paul, still languishing in prison and nearing the end of his life, with only Luke as his companion, asks Timothy to come to him and writes, 'Get Mark and bring him with you, for he is useful in my ministry' (2 Timothy 4.11). Whatever the pros and cons of Mark's original failure, when Paul eventually gave him a second chance, he didn't fail again.

There is one further and very significant mention of Mark in the New Testament, and that is in connection with Peter. As he concludes his first letter, written from Rome to mainly Gentile believers scattered throughout Asia Minor, Peter says, 'Your sister church . . . sends you greetings; and so does my son Mark' (1 Peter 5.13). 'My son Mark' – what a super epithet for one who had been deemed a failure, but then Peter knew from experience what it meant to be a failure!

The term may very well be one of intimacy and indebtedness. Mark, as the son of Mary in whose house the early church in Jerusalem met for worship, would have known, and been known by, Peter from those early days. There was clearly a close personal relationship, which the older man appreciated and described in family terms.

But it may also have been a term of indebtedness. Those who have worked in demanding leadership roles are well aware of the value of personal assistants. They are never in the limelight, rarely getting the credit for what they do, but their contribution to the work of the leader is invaluable. It was this kind of backroom support that Mark offered to Paul and, in a very special way, to Peter.

There is impressive evidence that Mark became Peter's interpreter, and that much of the Gospel that bears his name is a record of what Peter preached and taught about Jesus. Probably the earliest of the four Gospel records, it has all the characteristics of an eye-witness account of the life and ministry of Jesus. Written in rough Greek, Mark's Gospel seems to take us, with great rapidity, from one event or story to another, leaving us breathless with fear and excitement. There is action on every page. Realism and simplicity combine to present a powerful testimony to Jesus, the Son of God. Almost certainly written in the 60s, when the martyrdom of Christians was at its height, it was a glorious witness to Jesus, the chief of martyrs who 'gave his life as a ransom for many' (Mark 10.45). Mark's Gospel has brought glory to God and been a source of inspiration and encouragement to the Church throughout the centuries.

Failure redeemed

What a transformation had taken place in the life of that young man who had returned home as a failure! He had become a valued associate of the two great leaders of the early Church, and the author of a Gospel that tells a graphic and compelling story of the life, death and resurrection of Jesus.

There is something of eternal significance here for all of us, because at some stage in life we all experience failure. What we learn from the story of Mark is that failure need not have the last word. There is a way back. Failure can be redeemed.

I can't help feeling that this is one of the reasons why Peter used such an endearing and intimate expression as 'my son' when referring to Mark. For he too had failed, as indeed had all the disciples – much more drastically and dramatically than Mark. In the shadow of the cross they had abandoned Jesus, and Peter had also denied him with oaths and curses. That's one of the reasons why they were so distraught at his death. It had left them in a vacuum, with all the loose ends of memory, guilt, and a sense of moral failure.

But failure didn't have the last word. The risen Jesus appeared to them in the upper room, gave them his peace, breathed on them his Spirit and sent them out into the world to spread the good news. He didn't say of their desertion and denial, 'I told you so.' He didn't extract from them a promise of a better performance next time. His peace and recommissioning, like his love, was without strings. Failure had been redeemed.

It was that thought which stood me in good stead on one particular occasion when faced with a major challenge in my ministry. Though I was convinced that God wanted me to do this demanding task for him, I hesitated. I needed to resolve something within myself before I said 'Yes' to God. In my private devotions I had been using the following words of a famous hymn as an act of dedication:

Be our strength in hours of weakness,
In our wanderings be our guide;
Through endeavour, failure, danger,
Father, be thou at our side.

Love Maria Willis (1824–1908)

In facing the new task, I knew that endeavour would not be a problem. To use a modern expression, I would give it my best shot. The nature of the task would bring increased strain, so danger was a real possibility to someone with serious heart disease. But, strangely enough, I was not in the least anxious about that. It was the issue of failure that caused my hesitation. Was I prepared to undertake the task even if it meant failure on my part? It wasn't until I was able, with complete sincerity, to answer 'Yes' to that question, that my hesitation disappeared to be replaced with the joy of obedience.

It wasn't a response based on emotion, but a conviction based on truth. Mark had discovered that failure can be redeemed. Peter and the other disciples had been amazed, humbled and transformed by the same truth. Indeed, it seemed that the experience of failure had made them better equipped for the task God had committed to them.

Of course, it would be foolish to glory in failure, but it would be unwise to despise it. After all, in the eyes of the world, our Lord was a public failure. Yet he didn't try to hide that fact, nor did he try to sanitize or fantasize it. In the face of it he persisted in trusting a God who might let him down, let him suffer, let him die. He refused to let go of his Father, even when his Father seemed to have let go of him (Mark 15.34; Luke 23.46). He knew that failure need not be the last word. The whole thrust of his ministry and message was that failure could be redeemed. But more than that, he was, himself, the failure who redeemed, the universal victim who provided the way back to God.

6

≈

Stephen
who said the right thing
at the wrong time

A friend of mine was warmly commending the competence of one of our senior church leaders. 'He always says the right thing at the right time,' he commented. And then, with a naughty twinkle in his eye, he added, 'I hope that one day he might say the right thing at the wrong time!' It was a shrewd, if humorous, observation. In the context of our conversation, it was a gentle plea for a radical confrontation with the Establishment, a willingness to 'rock the boat' in the cause of justice, a preparedness to become unpopular for the sake of truth.

History is littered with the powerful and prophetic utterances of such people; indeed, sometimes history has been shaped by them. The Church and society would be the poorer without them. They are what my friend called 'profitable inconveniences', forcing us to grapple with thorny issues that we might wish to ignore or sweep under the carpet.

An unlikely inconvenience

Stephen, unexpectedly, proved to be just such a disturber of the status quo. It cost him his life. But the Church of Jesus Christ was never the same again. And it all began as a result of a domestic crisis in the Jerusalem church.

There were two distinct groups within that church: the Hebrews, who used the Aramaic language, and the Hellenists, so-called because they spoke only Greek. The Hebrew Christians, who had always lived in Palestine, had wisely continued the Jewish tradition of offering care to the needy, especially women who had been widowed. The Hellenists, having lived beyond Palestine for generations, had returned to settle in Jerusalem. Many of them had responded to the preaching of the early Christian believers, and were a significant group within the Jerusalem church. They felt, however, that *their* widows were being discriminated against, because they were being denied help from the common fund for the relief of the poor. 'The Hellenists complained against the Hebrews because their widows were being neglected in the daily distribution of food' (Acts 6.1).

In a society where girls married quite young, often to older husbands, the number of widows was increasing. So the problem was a pressing one. It was disturbing the unity of the rapidly growing Christian community and needed to be resolved.

The twelve apostles wisely and quickly got to grips with the situation. They made it clear that domestic administrative matters should not be allowed to distract them from their primary task of proclaiming and teaching the gospel: 'It is not right that we should neglect the word of God in order to wait at tables' (Acts 1.2). But at the same time they saw the proper care of all widows as being consistent with that gospel, and made provision for it. They invited the whole community of disciples to choose seven men from among their number and, laying their hands upon them with prayer, the apostles commissioned them for the task. Stephen, it seemed, was top of their shortlist.

He, like the other six, fulfilled the criteria the apostles had laid down, of being 'men of good standing, full of the Spirit and of wisdom' (Acts 6.3). On the surface, it seemed an unnecessarily high qualification for 'waiting on tables', but it was an indication of the importance the apostles placed on the pastoral care of widows. But that wasn't to be their only occupation, for Stephen, and some of the others, would also be used by God to take the word of the gospel beyond the borders of Jerusalem.

And God had even more significant plans for this particularly gifted man.

A spokesman for God

Chosen and commissioned to wait at tables, Stephen suddenly found himself the centre of controversy. He wasn't the first to discover that doing God's work in God's way could rub some people up the wrong way. Stephen, 'full of grace and power, did great wonders and signs among the people' (Acts 6.8), and not everyone was pleased. Some were very annoyed and said so. They shared Stephen's Hellenistic background, but that didn't stop them having a go at him for daring to undermine their religion and livelihood.

Many of them had returned to Jerusalem to retire, and found the presence and prestige of the temple to be a source of pride and security to them. They must have felt betrayed when this upstart convert to Christianity began speaking against the temple and the law – especially when he used the synagogue platform to do so! 'This man never stops saying things against this holy place and the law' (Acts 6.13). They had argued with him but couldn't withstand the power of Stephen's Spirit-filled wisdom. In response they paraded their prejudices as principles, resorted to false witnesses, manipulated the crowds and had Stephen hauled before the Sanhedrin, the Jewish council.

At that point they let slip the real issue that was at stake in their charge against Stephen. It had crystallized into Jesus versus the temple. 'We have heard him say that this Jesus of Nazareth will destroy this place and will change the customs that Moses handed on to us.' But it was all a misinterpretation of the actual words of Jesus (John 2.19–21), which Stephen had probably been expounding in the synagogue. However, they were in no mood to listen to reasoned argument.

The temple would eventually suffer destruction, not at the hands of Jesus, but as a consequence of Jerusalem's failure to recognize the day of God's visitation (Luke 19.41–48). It was this understanding of history that Stephen had the courage to share with them. In connection with the description of Stephen as 'full of the Holy Spirit and wisdom', Professor James Dunn comments that the full phrase 'envisages one whose inspiration, insight and maturity was exceptionally well matured' (Dunn, 1996). Stephen saw that the temple must pass away, that the law was but a stage towards the gospel and that Jesus was the reality to which temple and law pointed. It was a devastating message. Small wonder it provoked such harsh reaction – a reaction that would not have been helped by the look on Stephen's face! 'And all who sat in the council looked intently at him, and they saw that his face was like the face of an angel' (Acts 6.15).

A brave storyteller

When Stephen was invited by the high priest to give an answer to the accusations levelled against him, he didn't nail his colours firmly to the fence. If he had done so he might have saved his life. But no! The truth of Christianity was at stake and he wasn't prepared to compromise. The accusations against him had been somewhat garbled. His response to them was clear and clinical. He knew the power of story in recalling Israel's early history and told it perceptively and fearlessly (Acts 7.1–60).

He told the familiar story which his listeners knew well. There were people in that council who were experts at telling it in its traditional form. They were bulwarks of the official version. But Stephen told the old story in a new way – and they were furious. He was a man full of the Holy Spirit. He therefore told it from the Holy Spirit's perspective. He was able to tell the story from an angle, which came to light after the Holy Spirit had helped the Church to see that the cross and resurrection of Jesus had been God's plan from eternity.

Given that in our day some Christians can get upset if they're asked to sing a well-known hymn to an unfamiliar tune, I can imagine Stephen's hearers veering towards apoplexy as the old, old story was given a new twist! And it got worse as the full implication of what he was saying dawned upon them.

They heard him declare that the presence of God was not tied to a holy land nor a holy building. 'Solomon built a house for him. Yet the most high does not dwell in houses made by human hands' (Acts 7.47–48). They listened to him speak of their patriarchs who, unlike them, were prepared to launch out and take risks rather than be guardians of the status quo. Most telling of all, perhaps, was the implication that in rejecting and crucifying Jesus, they had continued the policy which they had followed throughout their national history. 'You stiff-necked people, uncircumcised in heart and ears, you are forever opposing the Holy Spirit, just as your ancestors used to do' (Acts 7.51–53).

From this point onwards, there seemed no possibility of avoiding 'blood on the carpet'. His next words, however, signed his death warrant. As they ground their teeth at him, Stephen, filled with the Holy Spirit, gazed into heaven and saw the glory of God and Jesus standing at the right hand of God. 'Look', he said, 'I see the heavens open and the Son of Man standing at the right hand of God!' (Acts 7.54–56).

He had said the right thing at the wrong time. It was those words and that vision that lit the blue touchpaper of their anger and prejudice. They could no longer contain their fury. Mob psychology took over. They didn't even wait for a verdict to be given, but dragged him outside the city and began to stone him. Their coats, which they had removed to make easier the throwing of stones, 'they laid at the feet of a young man named Saul' (Acts 7.58).

The end and the beginning

Stephen's vision of the opened heaven and the sight of Jesus, a crucified criminal, standing in such an exalted position at God's right hand, may have been more than his enemies could stand – but it was a source of consolation and hope to one who stood on the threshold of martyrdom. Stephen was about to become the victim of a religious mob, who believed they were serving God in stoning him to death. What an encouragement, therefore, for him to see another victim, Jesus the crucified and risen victim, standing in the place of honour beside his Father.

The content of Stephen's vision was an endorsement of his way of life. His life as a Christian disciple was motivated by the crucified, risen and ascended Christ. His retelling of the story before the Jewish council had been inspired by seeing it, as it were, through the eyes of Jesus the victim, rather than through the eyes of those who, in violence, rejected him. The gospel he preached was a gospel of the opened heaven, with an accessible Father, at whose side stands the one who made such access possible.

Being filled with the Spirit, Stephen's life had been modelled on the life of Jesus, for it is a primary task of the Spirit to take of the things of Christ and reveal them to us (John 16.12–15). It is not surprising, therefore, that his death also reflected the death of Jesus. It was marked by rejection, suffering, trust in the face of death and prayer for his enemies. 'While they were stoning Stephen, he prayed, "Lord Jesus, receive my spirit." Then he knelt down and cried in a loud voice, "Lord do not hold this sin against them." When he had said this, he died' (Acts 7.59–60).

It marked the end and the beginning. It marked the end of Stephen's earthly life and ministry but, of much greater significance, it marked the beginning of a wider mission (Acts 8.1–2). The Greek-speaking Jews associated with Stephen's attack on the temple were expelled from Jerusalem, and began a wider mission that reached Judea and Samaria and even led to evangelism on the desert road to Egypt (Acts 8.26–40). The influence of Stephen had reached far beyond waiting at tables! Chosen to assist and take the pressure off the apostles, he didn't neglect that responsibility but, in the power of the Spirit, he transcended it, becoming a powerful witness to the risen Christ and helping to shape the history of the Christian Church.

7

❧

John the Baptist
who worked himself out of a job

'Why did you become a priest?' is a question I have been asked frequently. 'Sheer frustration' has always been my reply, and I can tell by the look on the faces of the questioners that it isn't the answer they had anticipated. Clearly, they had expected some kind of spiritual description of a heavenly call, and are quite put out by my earthly response. But an honest question requires an honest answer.

When the 'call' came I was serving as a lay minister, pastoring a small but growing Anglican congregation which met in a church building situated about half a mile from the parish church to which it was linked. Though permitted to teach and visit the people, my lay status disqualified me from taking baptisms, weddings and funerals, and officiating at services of Holy Communion. I could use all the hours God gave me to care for people but when it came to those pivotal points of human existence I stepped aside and let someone else, usually the local vicar, take over. It didn't bother me, but the more I cared for the congregation the more it began to bother them. They couldn't understand why, having offered them pastoral care, I had to take a back seat, as it were, when it came to the supreme moments of their sorrow or joy.

As time went by I became increasingly aware of a sense of incompleteness about my ministry, coupled with a growing feeling of frustration. The frustration reached boiling point on those few occasions when, having prepared the people, through the ministry of the Word, to receive Holy Communion, I had to send them home without it because the local vicar had forgotten to turn up!

I am not proud of my feelings of frustration but I believe it was the catalyst, together with the active encouragement of colleagues, that propelled me towards ordination. It is also the reason why John the Baptist has always been a source of challenge and inspiration to me. He knew how to cope with frustration. Throughout his unique and demanding ministry, even in the face of unjust imprisonment and cruel martyrdom, he triumphed over frustration – because Jesus, the one he was waiting for, not only turned up but lived up to his name! And, as the gospel story reminds us, Jesus and John are forever linked.

John the Baptist and Jesus of Nazareth were related through their mothers. There is no record that they ever met or spoke to one another as children. As adults, however, when their paths crossed in the Jordan Valley, it marked 'the beginning of the good news of Jesus Christ, the Son of God' (Mark 1.1).

John was the son of a priest, Jesus a humble assistant in his father's carpentry trade. By the time John appeared on the banks of the Jordan, he was already a notable figure within his community. His forthright and uncompromising preaching was backed by a lifestyle that was single-minded and austere. Bearing many of the characteristics of a latter-day Elijah, he couldn't be ignored. Jesus, on the other hand, emerged from virtual obscurity. He was unknown outside his home town of Nazareth. Their meeting by the river Jordan began a massive reversal of roles that saw John marginalized and Jesus thrust into the full glare of publicity.

But though John was to suffer an ignominious death at the hands of a foolish and cruel king Herod, he is forever remembered and honoured as the curtain-raiser to the supreme and saving ministry of Jesus Christ.

Born to prepare a way

'What are you going to be when you grow up?', has been the conventional question adults have asked young children throughout the ages. If that question was ever put to John, he must have had a hard time explaining his answer, for it seems his future role as the forerunner of God's Messiah was determined before he was born!

Elizabeth, his mother, would also have had some of her own explaining to do. She and Zechariah had been praying for a child but without success. She was barren and they were both getting on in years. It seemed hopeless. But God intervened, a son was promised and they were to call him John. They were also given an outline of his future life. He would be no ordinary child. The spirit and power of Elijah would be with him. He would cause many people to turn to the Lord and prepare the way for God's Messiah (Luke 1.5–17). Zechariah couldn't believe it, and said so – that is, before he was struck dumb. But eventually it happened, just as the messenger of God had promised. Elizabeth got the child she had prayed for, Zechariah got back the use of his tongue and praised the Lord with a prophecy that has resonated across the centuries ever since (Luke 1.57–80). It included this affirmation about what his son would be when he grew up: 'And you, child, will be called the prophet of the Most High; for you will go before the Lord to prepare his ways' (Luke 1.76).

Did John himself have any say in the matter? Was he condemned always to have someone else pull the strings? Did he feel his arm was being twisted by his mother and father? Perish the thought! Yet it isn't hard to imagine that there must have been times in that household when there was the possibility of a mini-rebellion, as John, given his fiery temperament, felt hemmed in by a predetermined plan for his future.

As later events proved, John was his own man, a fact not inconsistent with his being filled with the Holy Spirit, even in the womb. John was his own man, but it was the Spirit who made him what he was. The Spirit does not obliterate personality or reduce everyone and everything to the lowest common denominator. On the contrary, he enhances and enriches personality. The work of the Spirit is to make us more truly human. It was the Spirit who was preparing him, with all his complex and creative humanity, to prepare the way of the Lord.

I believe that accounts for the content and power of his preaching and the amazing response of the people to it (Mark 1.5). His was no comfortable message. People were challenged to return to God, and to show they were sincere by a radical change of lifestyle. Tax-collectors were given strong advice about how to conduct their business and soldiers were warned against taking bribes. The social implications of his message were loud and clear; there was no room for evasion and few, if any, were let off the hook (Luke 3.7–14). It was a universal call to 'a baptism of repentance for the forgiveness of sin' (Mark 1.4). The matter was urgent, the kingdom was at hand and the King was about to knock at the gates.

One more powerful than I

John was not only a fiery preacher; he was also a skilled and faithful one. His dramatic Elijah-like appearance, all hair and leather, his scathing denouncements, 'you brood of vipers', and his call to repentance, certainly drew the undivided attention of the crowds (Matthew 3.1–11). But he didn't allow their attention to become fixed on him. He raised the level of expectancy even further by declaring himself to be only the forerunner of their long-expected Messiah. Even before Jesus appeared on the scene, he began to direct the enthusiasm of the crowds away from himself to Christ. 'The one who is more powerful than I is coming after me; I am not worthy to stoop down and untie the thong of his sandals. I have baptized you with water; but he will baptize you with the Holy Spirit' (Mark 1.6–8). The process of working himself out of a job had begun!

That process gathered pace when Jesus approached John and, despite John's embarrassment, asked for baptism at his hands. And the process took a great surge forward on the day when, as he was telling the crowds about the one who was coming, he saw Jesus walking towards him. At the sight of Jesus, I doubt if John could keep the excitement out of his voice or his hands by his side as he cried, in words that linked the coming of Jesus with their nation's great deliverance at the Exodus, 'Here is the Lamb of God who takes away the sin of the world' (John 1.29).

There must have been a deep sense of satisfaction in the heart of John as Jesus appeared among them. After all, it was for this moment he was born. It was for this he had been trained and prepared. At last he had the visual aid for his preaching. The expectation he had created was being fulfilled. 'The one more powerful than I' had arrived.

But the next day that sense of satisfaction must have been tinged with a touch of realism, as the practical implications of the arrival of Jesus became apparent. John was standing with two of his disciples as Jesus was again walking by. Again John declared, 'Look, here is the Lamb of God.' This time, however, two of John's disciples left him to follow Jesus and stay with him (John 1.35–42).

We don't know what thoughts were in John's mind as he watched his two disciples disappear down the road with Jesus. Along with a balanced feeling of satisfaction and realism, there might very well have been a sense of loss. The support and companionship of friends and colleagues is something to be treasured. Often, we only fully appreciate it when it is taken from us. I doubt if John was above such natural feelings of loss, and even if he was his friends simply would not allow him to ignore the fact that he was losing disciples to Jesus (John 3.26; 4.1). But whatever his personal feelings, he had the perfect answer to their queries.

The bridegroom's friend

His answer consisted of a series of graphic images that left them in no doubt about how he saw his role in relation to Jesus.

As ever, John was forthright and specific in his response. To the request from the religious authorities to identify himself, he didn't prevaricate. 'I am not the Messiah', he said with firmness (John 1.20–21); and went on to assure them that he was neither Elijah, who was to proclaim the dreadful Day of the Lord (Malachi 4.5), nor the prophet, who would speak the word of God to the people (Deuteronomy 18.15–28). In other words, he didn't fit their preconceived categories. If he had done so, they would have known how to deal with him. They were puzzled, and persisted in their demand to know who he was. So he provided them with two images to help clarify his role.

He described himself as a voice. 'I am the voice of

one crying out in the wilderness. "Make straight the way of the Lord," as the prophet Isaiah said.' He was the voice of scripture, the voice of the prophet Isaiah (Isaiah 40.3). Unlike Isaiah, however, he was not preparing a road for God's people to return to the promised land, but for God to come to his people in the person of Jesus Christ. As Raymond E. Brown has commented, 'His baptizing and preaching in the desert was opening up the hearts of men, levelling their pride, filling their emptiness, and thus preparing them for God's intervention' (Brown, 1971).

John, it seems, was saying to them, 'Look, I just have a walk-on part in this drama. Don't try and categorize me, you must listen to the voice.'

His second image, that of the 'friend of the bridegroom', was even more explicit regarding his role in relation to Jesus. It arose out of the observation that Jesus was now baptizing and 'all were going to him' (John 3.22–30). Some saw it as a threat to John's ministry and influence. John saw it not only as a natural and welcome development, but also as a source of deep joy. He was not the bridegroom, nor a rival to the bridegroom, nor was he there to attract the bride; he was simply the friend of the bridegroom. In today's terminology, he was the best man, the one charged to assist in the arrangements for the wedding, and then to fade out of the picture as the bridegroom stepped forward to meet the bride. It is a superb image of John's perception of his task as the forerunner of the Messiah. It took a special kind of person to fulfil such a role. John was that person, a man with the ability to be a number one, but ready and immensely able to function as a number two. He summed up the task so wonderfully well when he said, 'He must increase, but I must decrease.'

Great expectations

All too soon, however, John's claim that he 'must decrease' became devastatingly true. In the most dramatic and cruel circumstances, he was to prove the reality of his commitment to promote the cause of Christ and suffer the consequences.

His fearless witness to God's right way of living attracted the crowds but got him into serious trouble. He didn't mince his words, nor did he tone them down for the privileged classes. In his forthright call to a baptism of repentance, he had challenged others to stand up and be counted. Now, he practised what he preached and put his head on the block, literally, by condemning Herod Antipas for blatant adultery (Mark 6.14–29). Herod had married Herodias, his brother's wife, and John told him firmly, 'It is not lawful for you to have your brother's wife.' Understandably, Herod was a bit put out and had John arrested and imprisoned. It was the beginning of the end of what had been, by any standards, a remarkable public ministry.

It was in prison that John had his darkest hour. He was assailed by doubt regarding the status and mission of Jesus, and sent his disciples with the poignant question, 'Are you the one who is to come, or are we to wait for someone else?' (Matthew 11.3). Had John lost the plot? No. But he was puzzled. His expectations were taking a knock. Loneliness and isolation, following hard on the heels of energetic and popular success, would cause most of us to get things temporarily out of perspective. John was no exception.

He had specifically prophesied that the Messiah would bring judgement: 'The axe is already at the root of the tree' (Matthew 3.7–12). But as he languished in prison, the victim of evil and injustice, there was no sign of the judgement he expected. The powers that be were, literally, getting away with murder. And though part of the Messiah's brief was 'to proclaim liberty to the captives, and release to the prisoners' (Isaiah 61.1), he remained unreleased and, as far as we are aware, unvisited by Jesus.

It is a measure of his trust in Jesus, however, that he asked the question. And Jesus revealed his trust in John by the manner in which he answered it. 'Go and tell John what you hear and see: the blind receive their sight, the lame walk, the lepers are cleansed, the deaf hear, the dead are raised, and the poor have good news brought to them. And blessed is anyone who takes no offence at me' (Matthew 11.4–6). To put it another way, 'Happy is the person who is not offended by the unconventional and unexpected way in which God does his work.'

It was a message directed at John's uncertainty. John clearly expected a Messiah who would sort things out, even if it meant blood on the carpet. Jesus had his own way of sorting things out. God's judgement doesn't always operate by wielding a big stick. In Jesus it was the opening of a big heart of love and compassion. The Messiah's power is not demonstrated by battering everyone into submission but by the persuasiveness of invincible love.

We must allow God to do his work in his own way. The vision of the kingdom and rule of God is the hope that inspires us and we catch glimpses of it from time to time, but as we await its full realization we experience the continuation of evil, suffering and death. It is the paradox with which Christians in all ages have had to live.

It was the paradox with which John had to die. An adulterous and weak king, a scheming woman and a dancing girl combined to bring about his ignominious death in the loneliness of Herod's forbidding fortress of Machaerus. He could decrease no further (Matthew 14.1–12).

Greatest and least

John the Baptist's mission was unique. So also was the tribute Jesus paid to him (Matthew 11.7–20). He was no waverer, bending like a reed in the wind. He was no hypocrite, no dressed-up flatterer of kings. He was God's prophet, the last one before the Messiah, specially chosen to prepare the way of the Lord (Malachi 3.1). As such, Jesus said of him, 'Truly I tell you, among those born of women no one has arisen greater than John the Baptist; yet the least in the kingdom of heaven is greater than he' (Matthew 11.11).

Those words take nothing from our Lord's praise of him, for they echo what John himself recognized. Instead, they add to the significance of his role as the forerunner of the Messiah. The paths of John and Jesus crossed at the river Jordan, itself a significant crossing place in the history of Israel. It also proved to be a meeting place of great symbolism for the gospel. As the late Lord Blanch reminded us, 'John was the last representative of the old prophetic order. Jesus is the beginning of something new' (Blanch, 1988).

John worked himself out of a job by sticking to his task until it was completed – even though it meant death in captivity. In doing so, he prepared the way for one who, through death and resurrection, was released into all the world for all time to make all things new.

8

❧

Simeon and Anna
who belonged to the third age

The month of March 1993 is indelibly imprinted on
my memory. I had been charged with the onerous
responsibility of interviewing forty people, and to
make a recommendation regarding each that would
radically affect their lives. In prospect it was daunt-
ing. In reality it was a sheer delight – and my own life
was changed as a result.

The forty interviewees were all female deacons in
the Church of England. My task was to help test their
vocation to the priesthood. To be honest, I felt a little
uncomfortable, for together they represented hundreds
of years of godly, devoted and gifted ministry within
the church and society.

I reckoned that God had been testing their vocation
for years, and that the church had been testing his
patience and theirs for far too long! My immediate
task, therefore, required humility and sensitivity. So
I decided not to ask a series of questions but, instead,
to invite each of them to share with me the story of
their journey of faith. As I listened to and learned of
the grace of God at work through their lives, my heart

was uplifted and my own faith enlarged. I felt humbled and immensely privileged to be on the receiving end of such authentic priestly ministry.

Yet, even in the midst of such a wealth of Christian experience, one story stood out – that of an eighty-four-year-old Anglican nun. Many would have considered her to be long past her sell-by date, unsuitable for ordination to the priesthood and, metaphorically speaking, fit only to be put out to grass. God had other ideas.

The turning point came when, having outlined her past and present journey of faith, she said, with a wonderfully wicked twinkle in her eye, 'Bishop, may I share with you my vision for the future'! Suddenly I saw her not in terms of old age, and a gentle fading-away of usefulness, but as a member of the third age with a distinctive ministry to offer, based on experience, wisdom and faith. I recommended her for ordination to the priesthood and reckoned that Simeon and Anna were looking on with approval.

Purposeful ageing

The stories of Simeon and Anna are inserted within the story of Jesus (Luke 2.25–40), and are a source of encouragement and inspiration, especially to all those who are considered to be in the so-called twilight years of life. Simeon and Anna would have endorsed the sentiments of the poet Robert Browning, when he wrote,

> Grow old along with me
> The best is yet to be.

Certainly, it was in the closing years of their lives that they encountered their greatest joy and fulfilment. All too easily we dismiss those of mature age using labels such as pensioner, senior citizen or retired, and collude with the impression that they should be quietly shunted into the slow lane of life. I prefer the concept of the third age, that period of life when, having discharged those responsibilities of earlier years, we are liberated to enjoy a self-fulfilment that added years make possible. Simeon and Anna, however satisfying their earlier lives had been, were in no doubt that God had kept the best until last – something which he has a habit of doing (John 2.10)!

A man of vision

The Anglican nun shared her vision for the future with me. God shared his vision of the future with Simeon, together with a personal assurance about the timing of his death: 'It had been revealed to him by the Holy Spirit that he would not see death before he had seen the Lord's Messiah' (Luke 2.26).

Though we are not told the age of this man who suddenly appeared in the temple at a significant point in the life of Jesus, there are clear indications that he was an elderly priest who was still involved in the work of that holy place. What we do know for certain is that Simeon was a person noted for his religious uprightness (Luke 2.25). His behaviour was consistent with his belief. There was no gap between. Such an integrated life was made possible because 'the Holy Spirit rested on him'.

But there was one other vital ingredient in his character that made him the ideal person to welcome the infant Jesus on his first visit to the temple, namely that he was a man of hope. 'He was looking forward to the consolation of Israel.' He knew the promise of the scriptures, and was looking and waiting for the Messiah who would bring about God's restoration and redemption of his people (see Isaiah 40.1; 49.13; 51.3). Israel, the chosen nation in which he lived, had largely lost hope, having failed in its God-given task to be a light to the surrounding world. Ultimately, it would fail to recognize its Messiah.

Simeon's hope held firm. His faith was well founded. The shepherds required a sign in order to recognize the infant Jesus. Simeon was so in tune with God, and his expectancy, fostered by the scriptures, was so acute that he immediately recognized the status of the child presented to him in the temple. What an amazing happening that proved to be! An old man holds in his arms a six-week-old baby who is, at long last, 'the consolation of Israel'. An old man, ready to die, holds in his arms the child who would one day destroy death.

But this meeting between Simeon and the infant Jesus was not coincidental. The Holy Spirit is in the business of making significant connections, and under his impulse Simeon was on priestly duty in the temple at the appropriate moment. Mary and Joseph were there because the law required it. Forty days after the birth of a male child, the mother was required to come to the temple for purification. If the child was her first-born, the occasion was also used to present, or dedicate, him to God (Leviticus 12.1–8; Exodus 13.2, 12–16). As the priestly representative of God, Simeon received the child into his arms. Thus the Spirit and the law combined to facilitate the significant meeting, and produced, from the lips of Simeon, the inspired song:

> Master, now you are dismissing your
>   servant in peace,
>   according to your word;
> for my eyes have seen your salvation,
>   which you have prepared in the
>   presence of all peoples,
> a light for revelation to the Gentiles
>   and for glory to your people Israel.
>
> (Luke 2.29–32)

This wonderful song of praise, known as the *Nunc dimittis* (so called after the first two words in the Latin translation), has enriched the Church's worship of God across the centuries ever since.

A song of liberation

The theme of the song is liberation. Simeon sees himself as God's slave who, having faithfully looked forward to the coming of the Messiah, has, with his arrival, been honourably discharged from that task. It is the crowning moment of Simeon's life and work. He is now ready to die. But the arrival of the Messiah not only meant release for Simeon but also liberation for all people. His vision regarding this child is a universal one. It encompasses both Jew and Gentile. It speaks of salvation, or deliverance, for the whole world. Nor is the vision limited to so-called spiritual matters. Given that Israel was occupied by Roman armies at the time, there would have been those who would interpret his words in both political and social terms, seeing not only signs of hope but also clouds of conflict on the horizon.

This sense of ambiguity and contradiction is reinforced by Simeon's final words to Mary. 'This child is destined for the falling and rising of many in Israel, and to be a sign that will be opposed so that the thoughts of many will be revealed – and a sword will pierce your own soul too' (Luke 2.34–35). Thus the vision of glory contained in his song is balanced by the promise of pain in his words to Mary. Jesus Christ will bring deliverance – but at a cost.

It was not just a solemn note of warning; it was an amazing insight into the astonishing status and importance of this child who lay in his arms. He would make a difference in the world to which he came. God's Messiah would be a disturber of the status quo. He would bring peace but he would also create division. He would become a rock over which some would fall and on which others would stand. He would be a sign which some would receive and others would reject. His contact with people would face them with a crisis of decision. The destiny of people and of nations would be decided in relation to this child.

Clearly, Jesus Christ was going to be an uncomfortable person to have around. Just as the coming of light creates shadows, so the presence of Jesus, the light, truth and love of God, would introduce reality into every situation. His holiness would expose every sin and challenge every falsehood. Small wonder he was pushed out of the world he came to redeem. The powers that be couldn't cope with the intensity of his light and love. They made him a victim, nailed him to a cross – and pierced the soul of his mother at the same time.

Anna, a woman of character

There must have been something wonderfully reassuring to Mary and Joseph at the sudden appearance and ministry of Anna in the temple at that very moment. She was able to confirm the exalted vision of Jesus given by Simeon and, as a woman who had endured pain herself, she must also have been a source of comfort and strength to Mary, as she contemplated the meaning of the sword that would pierce her soul. Anna was the right person in the right place at the right time, which is not surprising, given the priorities of her life.

She was a godly woman of great age. After only seven years of marriage, she felt the pain of personal grief in the death of her husband. She never married again, but gave herself completely to the service of God and, like my friend the Anglican nun, was still going strong at the age at eighty-four! 'She never left the temple but worshipped there with fasting and prayer night and day' (Luke 2.37).

To modern ears that may sound a little intense and

rather fanatical, depicting someone who perhaps was out of touch with the real world. It would be a mistake to presume that Anna was any of these things. Her words and her actions revealed that she was both in touch with the world and in tune with what God was doing in it. Luke's words mustn't be pressed so far as to mean that she slept in the temple or, indeed, that she never slept at all, but was always worshipping, fasting and praying! No, the image that Luke conveys is of a person whose life is fully taken up with the worship and service of God. Every aspect of life was drawn towards that ultimate purpose. But far from cutting her off from the so-called real world, such a disciplined life of waiting upon God gave her the insight to grasp what was needed in her nation and how God was responding to it. It also helped her to recognize the child of Mary as the redeemer of the world.

My experience, gained over many years, of those who serve God as nuns and monks, is that they have a refreshing view of the world and its people. They often have those combined gifts from God of humility and humour that enable them to help those under pressure to get things into perspective.

Anna certainly did that. And she did it with evangelistic zeal. Not only did she confirm to Mary and Joseph the message of Simeon concerning the status of their son, she also spread the word. She 'began to praise God and to speak about the child to all who were looking for the redemption of Israel.' She gave thanks to God and witnessed to the people. That is why she spent so much time in the temple. She wasn't, as it were, keeping in with God and building up merit for the afterlife. She was fulfilling her calling as a prophetess, who was gifted by God to reveal his will to his people. Her great age didn't disqualify her from such a task but simply enhanced it.

Autumn years

Simeon and Anna were, to use a familiar expression, in the autumn years of life. But they saw those years in positive terms, having value and meaning in their own right. It was a period of life just as important and authentic as childhood, adolescence or early middle age.

Those of us who consider ourselves to be part of the third age do well to follow their example and conviction. Far from seeing the autumn years in negative terms as the melancholy season, we need to view them positively in terms of adventure, discovery and achievement. Autumn is a season of colour and beauty, with swirling flames of yellow and red and orange. Oh, yes! Autumn leaves finally fall to dust – but not before they have freely and gaily danced in the wind. Simeon and Anna kept dancing to great effect!

9

Priscilla and Aquila
who offered hospitality and more

I stood waiting patiently in the cold draughty doorway of a Victorian church in the week before Christmas. I wasn't waiting for Godot but for Santa Claus, who eventually arrived, in duplicate – a young married couple driving a Volvo Estate. They came as messengers bearing gifts from a wealthy and caring suburban congregation. At their church's toy service the previous Sunday, children and parents had brought gifts that were to be given to the poorer children of my inner-city parish. They had been sensitive and generous, for the car was overflowing not with broken and discarded toys but with new and imaginative gifts for children of all ages. The adults in my congregation were visibly moved by the quality of the gifts, and at their Christmas Eve party the children were thrilled to bits with their surprise presents.

And God had a surprise gift for me as well! The young couple who had delivered the gifts didn't dash back to suburbia as quickly as possible, their good deed done for the day. No. They stayed and took time to discover a little of the work we were trying to do in that needy area, and later committed themselves to supporting my wife and me in our missionary task. It was a partnership that brought the open hospitality of their home and their dedicated and practical assistance in the gospel work we were doing. They shared our joys and sorrows, standing alongside us in difficulty, understanding the pressures we faced, and offering the encouragement and affirmation so vital to our work. Like so many other similar couples, whose love for God and commitment to the work of the gospel have enriched and enabled our ministry, they were a gift from God. And though I say it humbly, I reckon that no less a person than St Paul himself would say 'Amen' to that, for he received a similar gift in the shape of Priscilla and Aquila.

St Paul had a distinguished missionary career. As far as he was concerned, it was all due to the grace of God, and he was right. But there were other factors. He was well equipped for the task. His preaching was powerful, his debating skill was considerable, his strategy was sound and his faith was resilient. And then there were Priscilla and Aquila.

In assessing Paul's career as the great missionary to the Gentile world, we would be guilty of a serious omission if we ignored the influence of this ordinary Christian couple with an extraordinary capacity for friendship. Their partnership with Paul proved to be of immense significance in the cause of the gospel. They had a special affinity with him and undoubtedly there was a warm bond between them.

Birds of a feather

Aquila and Priscilla (or Prisca as she is sometimes called) lived in Rome. Aquila was a Jew and his wife almost certainly a Jewess. One is not mentioned without the other in scripture, though since Priscilla's name is usually placed before her husband's, some have inferred that she came from a higher social class. More likely, perhaps, is that she was the dominant partner in their tent-making business. By the time they met up with Paul at Corinth, they had become Christians. They were active and influential members of the church in Rome, but had to leave that city in a hurry – expelled by the emperor's decree!

Emperor Claudius was fed up with the continual public squabbles among the large Jewish community in Rome, and he told them all to leave (Acts 18.2). What evidence there is seems to suggest that the preaching of Jesus as the Messiah was the cause of the disturbances. The Christian Jews were not prepared to desist and argued their cause with passion. But Claudius' patience was exhausted. He pinpointed the chief troublemakers on both sides of the divide and, in modern parlance, showed them the red card! Among those expelled were Aquila and Priscilla, who made their way to Corinth.

As later events proved, when it came to contending for the faith, they were not 'shrinking violets'. In this regard they certainly had an affinity with Paul, whose own record of disputing for the faith is well documented: 'He argued in the synagogue with the Jews and devout persons, and also in the market place

every day with those who happened to be there' (Acts
17.17). They clearly were on the same wavelength as
Paul in powerfully presenting the claims of Jesus the
Messiah.

But they not only shared Paul's approach to the
faith and its propagation, they were also skilled in the
same craft, that of tent-making. The fact that they
owned a house large enough to host the local church
(Romans 16.5) indicates that they probably ran a substantial leather-working business. They may even have
provided Paul with a job and a living wage to help him
keep body and soul together, for, on principle, he was
determined not to sponge on his converts (Acts 20.34).
Most important, they offered him the hospitality of
their home and the encouragement and support of
their friendship. 'Paul went to see them, and, because
he was of the same trade, he stayed with them, and
they worked together' (Acts 18.3).

To evangelize the city of Corinth and to cope with
the vibrancy and diversity of the young Corinthian
church was the demanding challenge that Paul faced
day by day. In such circumstances, the value of the
hospitality and friendship of Priscilla and Aquila
would have been immeasurable. Those of us who
have found ourselves at the cutting edge of work for
the kingdom of God know only too well the pressures that such ministry can bring. Paul, for instance,
outlined his experience of some of them when he
wrote, 'We are afflicted in every way, but not crushed;
perplexed, but not driven to despair; persecuted, but
not forsaken; struck down but not destroyed' (2
Corinthians 4.8–10).

There have been times when I, like many others, have known pressures which, though different from Paul's, have been almost unbearable. In the circumstances, it is vital to have a base of love, friendship and warm hospitality to which to return and regroup, as it were, at such times. Often our ministry on 'the edge' is only possible because of the back-up we receive from people like Priscilla and Aquila. That's why Paul spoke so warmly of them.

More than mere hosts

But Paul's high regard for the couple was not simply because they offered him a home and a job. Their contribution to the work of the kingdom of God was in every sense more extensive than that. As well as being committed Christians, they were well-to-do business folk. Their financial resources and their business interests enabled them to travel widely, and they used the opportunity to be with Paul and support his evangelistic work. It seems that their business travels often coincided with Paul's. That was almost certainly the case in Ephesus, where Paul had journeyed to from Corinth.

Ephesus was the capital of Asia and an important religious and commercial centre. It had a large Jewish population. It was, therefore, a very strategic place for mission and for business. It was while they were in Ephesus that they engaged in a very special piece of work in connection with a man called Apollos, from Alexandria. He later became a prominent, if somewhat ambivalent, figure in the early Church. He was an immensely gifted and able person, bubbling over with life and enthusiasm. He had a way with words and was wonderfully persuasive. 'He was an eloquent man, well-versed in the scriptures. He had been instructed in the Way of the Lord; and spoke with burning enthusiasm and taught accurately the things concerning Jesus, though he knew only the baptism of John' (Acts 18.24–25).

Priscilla and Aquila heard him preaching boldly in the local synagogue and were impressed – but concerned. They recognized in Apollos a person who was already showing signs of becoming a mighty advocate for the gospel. His power, eloquence and knowledge was plain for all to see, as was the evidence of the Spirit upon him, but they discerned certain deficiencies that needed to be put right. He needed further instruction.

We are not told specifically what those deficiencies were, but there are good grounds for believing that Apollos' knowledge of Jesus was not wholly accurate. Professor James Dunn suggests that 'his knowledge of Jesus came from reports of Jesus' ministry prior to his death and resurrection' (Dunn, 1996). There were obvious gaps in his understanding. But whatever the nature of these deficiencies, Priscilla and Aquila graciously and sensitively rectified them. After they had heard him speak in the synagogue, 'they took him aside and explained the Way of God to him more accurately' (Acts 18.26).

Those words provide a wonderful insight into the extraordinary ministry of this godly Christian couple. There is no evidence that they confronted him in public about his shortcomings. Doubtless, following their normal pattern of warm hospitality, they invited him to their home and there, in the privacy of that setting, exercised their ministry of explanation. They made good the gaps that existed in his understanding.

In later years, I am sure Apollos never ceased to thank God for the wise and sensitive ministry of Priscilla and Aquila. He would know that his own ministry was all the richer because of what they had taught him. I doubt if there is any Christian leader who has not experienced and appreciated a similarly sensitive ministry from modern-day Aquilas and Priscillas.

Imaginative teamwork

Paul certainly benefited from their consistent and committed ministry to him over several years. It is clear that he saw them as valuable members of his team, and although no one is literally indispensable, I reckon Priscilla and Aquila came fairly close to qualifying for that category. This was mainly because of the strategy Paul used in his work for the gospel. The formation of house churches was an important focus of community life in Paul's mission (Romans 16.5; 1 Corinthians 16.19; Colossians 4.15; Philemon 2). They, along with the larger gatherings of the whole community (1 Corinthians 11; 14; see also 16.2), were charismatic communities, local expressions of the body of Christ, in which gifts and ministries could be discovered and deployed for the mutual benefit of all. They were communities where people could not only unite in worship but also be made aware of their interdependence – they belonged to each other, and they needed each other, in Christ. Given the rich diversity of their fellowship and worship, they also had to come to terms with their need to maintain unity for the sake of Christ and the gospel. Divisions and partisanship often marred the unity of the early Corinthian church (1 Corinthians 3.1–9).

That was the context in which Priscilla and Aquila had to live and work. In Corinth, Ephesus and Rome, they used their financial resources to obtain houses large enough for the local church to meet in. Their affinity with Paul and their support for his strategy of making the house church the focus of community life made them key players in his team.

It also won them the admiration and commendation of Paul, who writes, in his letter to the Christians in Rome, 'Greet Prisca and Aquila, who work with me in Christ Jesus, and who risked their necks for my life, to whom not only I give thanks, but also all the churches of the Gentiles. Greet also the church in their house' (Romans 16.3–5a). The greeting is a testimony to the character and worth of Priscilla and Aquila. They were back in Rome again and still going strong, having earned the gratitude of Paul and of all the churches they had been associated with among the Gentiles.

There is a viewpoint in some quarters today suggesting that there is no need to say thank you to other Christians for sharing with us in the work of God. Clearly, it was not a viewpoint shared by Paul or the members of the Gentile churches. There is a ministry of gratitude and affirmation that we ought not to ignore, and Paul certainly didn't. Indeed, he shared with the church in Rome a remarkable and graphic insight into the ministry of Priscilla and Aquila when he referred to them as those 'who risked their necks for my life'. Not to have said thanks for such devoted service would have been churlish.

Tantalizingly, he doesn't enlarge on the incident in question. It may have occurred during the disturbances in Ephesus. It may well refer to an occasion when they attempted to use the influence their wealth and social position gave them to further Paul's mission. Whatever it was, they were prepared to make a stand and take the consequences. To be a member of Paul's mission team involved risk.

Integrated lifestyle

But in the case of Priscilla and Aquila, it also involved something more basic and ultimately more important. It can be summed up in a word – integration. There was a harmony and a wholeness about their lives which must have been a wonderful testimony to Christ and the gospel. It certainly provides us with an example to which we may aspire.

Their business life, social life and religious life seemed to gel together. It wasn't compartmentalized. There was no demarcation between the so-called sacred and secular aspects of life. They endorsed the earliest Christian creed, 'Jesus Christ is Lord', and proceeded to make good that profession in every aspect of life, in their home, their business, and their work of evangelism alongside Paul. They didn't neglect their business, travelling widely to maintain its success and influence. They didn't miss opportunities to witness, in Corinth, Ephesus and Rome, and wherever they lived their home became a church – but not only a church. It was also a place of community and social intercourse as well as a welcome haven, providing a listening ear for those in need of comfort, encouragement or godly advice.

Tucked away in my memory and in my prayers I have a roll of honour. On it are the names of many people, and couples, who throughout my life and work have been to me what Priscilla and Aquila were to Paul: ordinary people who, because of their love for God and their integrated lifestyle, have developed an extraordinary capacity to influence people across the business, social and religious spectra, for good. Unselfconsciously, they demonstrate the possibility of living a life that is broad in its interests, yet focused by a central conviction and motivation that serves to add lustre to every part of it.

It was an early Father of the Church, Irenaeus, who said, 'The glory of God is a human being fully alive.' Those who worked with Priscilla and Aquila or entered their home would have caught a glimpse of that glory.

10

Silas
who was a dependable companion

The spotlight that picks out the star of the show also, by the same token, casts other actors on the stage into shadow. Yet without those who play supporting roles, the show could not go on.

A similar truth penetrates virtually every dimension of public life. We see it in the world of politics, where media attention focuses on the words and actions of the official spokespersons and little, if any, attention is paid to those who work in the background. We see it in the world of sport, where high-flying teams and individuals are fêted, often worshipped, while those who offer invaluable assistance behind the scenes remain unknown and unsung. It also happens in the church today, and perhaps the work of a bishop provides a classic example. There was a time when the shepherd's crook he carried symbolized the entire nature of his task, namely to care for his flock – the clergy and people within his diocese. Today, however, while pastoral care remains the primary task, it seems that being chief pastor also includes the role of being chief executive of a large and costly institution.

I am only too well aware, from my own experience, of the excessive demands of a secular and multicultural society that requires church leaders to be media-competent and articulate spokespersons on a great variety of issues – education, politics, medical ethics, social deprivation and urban regeneration, to name but a few. The temptation to be a kind of 'rent a mouth' for the media needs to be avoided at all costs.

Nevertheless, there have been times, like the Bradford fire disaster, for instance, when one was required to articulate the sorrow of the community; or issues of social injustice, when one had to express the anger of the community and suffer the consequences. There have also been occasions of conflict within the church, where actions and decisions brought unavoidable hurt and threatened unity – the Church of England's decision to ordain women to the priesthood was a case in point.

Effective leadership in such challenging, and often stressful, situations becomes possible only with the help of able and dedicated people working with one and for one, usually in the background. Such help requires ability, humility and the integrity not only to give support but also to offer honest criticism.

When St Paul needed help in his missionary task he chose such a person, Silas by name, whose distinguished and dependable ministry was exercised in the shadow of Paul. He was cast in a supportive role, known principally as 'the companion of Paul'.

Chosen and graced

Nevertheless, Silas, or Silvanus, as he is sometimes called, was a gifted and highly regarded member of the Jerusalem church. He is first mentioned in connection with a problem that threatened to tear the early Church apart. The church in Jerusalem and the church in Antioch were at loggerheads. The main cause of the conflict concerned the place and importance of circumcision among converts to Christianity. Because of their Jewish background, those who had embraced Christianity and formed the church in Jerusalem saw circumcision as essential and non-negotiable. The Gentile converts of Antioch, however, were averse to such a suggestion and considered circumcision as unnecessary to salvation in Christ.

A General Church Council (Acts 15) was held in Jerusalem to address the issue, and Paul and Barnabas came to represent the view of the church in Antioch. It proved to be a most significant event in the life of the early church and crucial to the success of the mission of Christ. The momentous decision was taken not to impose circumcision on Gentile converts. It was no longer to be considered essential to salvation. James, who chaired the Council, summed up the discussion in these words: 'I have reached the decision that we should not trouble those Gentiles who are turning to God' (Acts 15.19). Barnabas and Paul went back to Antioch with the good news – and that's when Silas made his first appearance.

The Church Council in Jerusalem was sound in its judgement and wise in the manner in which it made it known to the Christians in Antioch. The members of the church in Jerusalem were not content to leave it to Barnabas and Paul to carry the news back. That would have been too easy and much less effective. Instead, they showed great sensitivity in sending two of their chief members, Judas and Silas, to go with Barnabas and Paul. They were to carry a letter setting out the details of the judgement. At the same time, they were to add their own testimony – thus putting flesh on the written word.

That was an astute move on the part of the Jerusalem church. It was unauthorized people from among their members who had caused the bother to the Christians at Antioch in the first place, so it seemed right to send authorized representatives to help put matters right. In Judas and Silas they sent two of their very best leaders. 'The apostles and the elders, with the consent of the whole church, decided to choose men from among their members and to send them to Antioch with Paul and Barnabas. They sent Judas called Barsabbas and Silas, leaders among the brothers' (Acts 15.22).

The Christians in Antioch soon discovered that Judas and Silas were not merely postmen with a good news letter from Jerusalem. They were prophets with the gift of teaching and exhortation. As they weren't in any hurry to get back home, they stayed with the church in Antioch and brought great encouragement and strength to its members. The healing quality of their ministry was in sharp contrast to the disruptive style of previous visitors from the church in Jerusalem. They stirred up trouble; Judas and Silas brought peace. 'After they had been there for some time, they were sent off in peace by the believers' (Acts 15.33).

After leaving Antioch, we never hear of Judas Barsabbas again. Silas, however, accepted a new responsibility as companion of Paul.

Taking the rough with the smooth

It was no easy assignment. Paul didn't suffer fools gladly. He could be quite tetchy on occasion, as Peter, Barnabas and Mark could testify. They all had differences of opinion with him. Indeed, it was Paul's refusal to have Mark as a companion on his missionary tour that left the way open for him to choose Silas instead. Together they set off on what is known as the Aegean mission – to those coasts that surrounded the Aegean Sea. *En route* they were joined by Timothy, who was to become an important member of Paul's team, with a much higher profile than Silas. Silas appeared committed to and content with a 'walk-on part' as Paul's companion.

As such, he would have been thrilled to share in ministry to the vibrant young churches, so that they were 'strengthened in the faith and increased in numbers daily' (Acts 16.5). It would have been a learning experience for him to note how Paul received the guidance of the Spirit, who closed two doors and opened a third, leading to Macedonia and eventually to Philippi. There, by the riverside, as Paul spoke to a group of women gathered at a Jewish place of prayer, 'the Lord opened the heart of Lydia', a wealthy business woman. As a result, she and her household were baptized (Acts 16.6–15).

Those were sunshine days for Silas as he watched and worked alongside Paul, but squalls were on the way. The gospel was about to cross swords with vested interests – always a hazardous experience!

It happened on the way to the place of prayer where they had first met Lydia. This time they met a woman of a different kind, from the other end of the social scale, an unfortunate slave-girl who had fallen into the hands of unscrupulous men and become a public spectacle. She was possessed by some form of evil spirit that caused her to make involuntary revelations and predict the future. Her owners had an eye to business. They cared more about profit than about her health and sanity. They used her as a fortune-teller and pocketed the proceeds.

For several days she persisted in pursuing Paul and his companions, crying out and giving unsolicited testimony as to who and what they were. Paul's patience eventually snapped. Turning to her in annoyance, he said to the spirit, 'I order you in the name of Jesus Christ to come out of her' – and it did. But then the balloon went up! 'When her owners saw that their hope of making money was gone, they seized Paul and Silas and dragged them into the market place before the authorities' (Acts 16.16–19). Other members of the mission team may have been around at that moment, but it was Paul and Silas who became the focus of anger and accusation. Clearly, Silas was identified as being Paul's right-hand man. As such, he also became the victim of prejudice.

The owners of the slave-girl were too shrewd to bring them before the city magistrates with the complaint, 'We was robbed!' They would have been given short shrift. No, they played the ancient, and modern, game of feeding the prejudices of the host community against ethnic minorities who practise peculiar customs. 'These men are disturbing our city; they are Jews and are advocating customs that are not lawful for us as Romans to adopt or observe.' Here was prejudice masquerading as principle. It is a game played not only across the world but also in our own nation today. I speak from personal experience.

The crowd reacted predictably, and the magistrates responded shamefully. The accusations were not investigated. Instead, judgement was pronounced, in the form of a public flogging and detention in the local prison. 'After they had given them a severe flogging, they threw them into prison and ordered the jailer to keep them securely' (Acts 16.23). A day that had begun with sunshine and a spring in the step ended in darkness and wounds on the back. Silas was discovering that to be a companion of Paul was a costly occupation, with no shortage of excitement.

The escapologists

That excitement took many forms. If Silas ever became a grandfather, the story of his dramatic escape from prison in Philippi would have become a firm favourite of his grandchildren. It certainly was an amazing happening. The earthquake that opened the prison doors was astonishing enough, but so was their ability, in the darkness of the dungeons, to pray and sing hymns to God at midnight. Since their prayer and praise came first, it seems that God didn't hang about with the answer. This time it didn't come by way of 'a still small voice' (1 Kings 19.12), but through the power of an earth tremor, that resulted in doors being opened and chains being loosed throughout the prison.

Clearly, Philippi prison was very much smaller than Wormwood Scrubs, for when the jailer, thinking all the prisoners had escaped, threatened to kill himself, Paul was able to stop the intended suicide with a shout of reassurance. 'Do not harm yourself, for we are all here.' The inmates were obviously few in number.

But if the duet of praise and earthquake at midnight were astonishing, they were matched by the amazing response of the jailer. Overwhelmed by the power of God's presence, he brought them out of prison and said, 'Sirs, what must I do to be saved?' Paul and Silas answered, 'Believe in the Lord Jesus, and you will be saved, you and your household.' He and his family received the word of the Lord. He tried to put right the wrong that had been done by washing their wounds. Then he and his whole family received that washing which comes from the wounds of Christ by being baptized (Acts 16.25–34).

But that wasn't the end of the matter. When morning came the magistrates, no doubt aware of the strange happenings at midnight, sent the police to the prison with instructions for their release. The magistrates wanted them 'to come out now and go in

peace'. 'Not on your life', was the gist of the reply.
Paul and Silas put fear into the magistrates by
reminding them that they were both Roman citizens,
and had been illegally and unfairly beaten and imprisoned. They refused to let the police hurry them away
quietly, and demanded that the magistrates put right
the wrong they had done. 'Let them come and take us
out themselves.' Paul and Silas won the day. The
magistrates 'came and apologized to them. And they
took them out and asked them to leave the city' –
glad to see the back of them, no doubt.

But it wasn't arrogance that produced the unyielding
attitude of Paul and Silas. It was perceptive pastoral
care. They were simply trying to protect the tiny
community of faith who lived in that city from any
similar prejudice-inspired attacks upon them. So the
last thing they did before leaving the city was to visit
the local Christian community. 'After leaving the
prison they went to Lydia's home; and when they had
seen and encouraged the brothers and sisters there,
they departed' (Acts 16.35–40). The care of the church
was their uppermost concern.

Companion of honour

They left the city behind, but not their trials nor their
joys. Indeed, the events in Philippi formed a pattern
that was repeated throughout their partnership in
mission. The work of evangelism and the growth of
local churches was intermingled with bitter opposition and threats to their lives. They did great work in
Thessalonica and Beroea, but had to be smuggled out

of those cities because of jealousy, prejudice and the rabble-rousing of a Jewish 'rent-a-mob' (Acts 17.1–16). Throughout the vicissitudes of life in the company of his more illustrious colleague, Silas remained a constant and dependable companion.

At first glance, it might appear difficult to quantify his significance within the story of the early Church. There are no recorded words of his to remember, no personal initiatives of note to recall, only a wonderful example of dependability which others saw, admired and welcomed. His home church saw it and commissioned him for a major diplomatic task (Acts 15.22–29). The churches he visited saw it and benefited greatly from his teaching and encouragement (Acts 15.30–34). Peter saw it and used him to scribe and perhaps shape his first letter, referring to him as a faithful (i.e. loyal and dependable) brother (1 Peter 5.12).

Supremely, however, it was Paul who saw it and chose him as his travelling companion. His judgement was not misplaced, for their partnership in the gospel held firm in every circumstance. Paul, it seems, couldn't bear to be parted from him for too long, for when circumstances separated them he sent instruction for Silas and Timothy to come to him as soon as possible (Act 17.14–15).

It was indicative of the bond between them, and it speaks volumes to today's church, where so many are content to serve in the background and whose greatest asset is dependability. This eloquent, gifted and faithful man, forever overshadowed by Paul, represents those multitudes of people that the Church of God cannot do without.

11

❧

Cornelius
who helped in the conversion of Peter

God believes in partnership. It is part of being God, and always has been.

We see it in the Old Testament where God used friends like Moses and Elijah, and enemies like Cyrus, king of Persia, to fulfil his purposes. Surprisingly, of the latter he said, 'He is my shepherd and he shall carry out my purpose' (Isaiah 44.28). We see it in the Gospels where Jesus frequently employed a 'do-it-yourself' strategy in connection with those he was helping. When healing the paralysed man, for instance, he asked for his cooperation: 'I say to you, stand up, take your mat and go to your home' (Mark 2.11). When feeding the multitude, he invited the assistance of his disciples, and used the contribution of loaves and fishes from an unnamed lad in the crowd (Mark 6.30–34). He sent his disciples out to proclaim the gospel, but worked alongside them as they did so – 'They went out and proclaimed the good news, while the Lord worked with them and

confirmed the message by the signs that accompanied it' (Mark 16.20).

Partnership is part of the character of God. He has
partners everywhere – including a huge inner-city
housing estate. Slum clearance had led to the demo-
lition of hundreds of houses and two Anglican church
buildings. The congregations of the latter were
thrilled when a new church was built to serve the
new estate – but there was a little difficulty. One
congregation was high church, the other was evan-
gelical, and neither wanted to let go of their tradition.
Many doubted that they could worship together or
that unity would be achieved. But, remarkably, it was,
and the congregation grew in strength and vitality.

Everyone played their part, but God had one special
partner in making it work. Ernie had come to faith
soon after he and his wife moved on to the estate.
They joined the new church soon after the building
was dedicated and as the two formerly separate congregations were exploring their new close relationship.
Ernie was the ideal person for that situation. He had
not been part of either congregation so he was not
hung up on any past tradition. Indeed, as a new
Christian with an enquiring mind, his questions,
which were guileless and inoffensive, challenged the
prejudices of others and in a strange way set them
free. They began to see that some particularly partisan
traditions were imprisoning them, stifling their
growth and outreach to the community. Added to
this was the undoubted impact of Ernie's Christian
life. His practical, uncluttered and attractive faith
clearly had the hallmark of reality and it opened up

the way to a forward movement in that church and community.

Another forward movement, but of far greater significance, took place in the first century AD, when God entered into partnership with a Roman soldier to facilitate one of the most boundary-breaking developments in the history of the Christian Church (Acts 10.1–48).

Double vision

Cornelius, a Roman centurion based at Caesarea, was one of two major players in that development. He was attracted to the Jewish faith. Tired of the various gods and widespread immorality of Roman society, he felt drawn to the One God and ethical purity of Judaism. He attached himself to the local synagogue and, though he was not ready to embrace the full menu of Jewish ritual and observance, his love for God and neighbour reflected the core of the Jewish faith. Prayer to God and concern for the practical needs of others was high on his list of priorities.

It seems that they were also high on God's list, for he responded to them in a most dramatic way. Cornelius was praying one afternoon when he had a vision of an angel of God coming to him and calling his name. To say that he was surprised would be an understatement – he was terrified, and said, 'What is it, Lord?' The angel answered, 'Your prayers and your alms have ascended as a memorial before God. Now send men to Joppa for a certain Simon who is called Peter; he is lodging with Simon, a tanner, whose house is by the seaside' (Acts 10.1–8). Cornelius did what he was told.

It is significant that the combination of 'prayer and alms' was what attracted God's attention and won his approval. There was a balance about Cornelius' devotion. His piety was horizontal as well as perpendicular. His love for God was not only expressed in his prayers but also in a practical love for his neighbour. No wonder he was so highly regarded by many Jewish people (Acts 10.22). That kind of integration between belief and behaviour carries an authenticity which is attractive to others. It was also the powerful combination that God used to fulfil his boundary-breaking purpose.

The other major player in the drama was Simon Peter. As the messengers from Cornelius approached the house in Joppa where he was lodging, he also was praying and receiving a vision from God. Unlike Cornelius, however, Peter wasn't terrified; he was downright annoyed, for the vision was both graphic and disturbing, going to the very heart of his religious identity. 'He saw the heaven opened and something like a large sheet coming down, being lowered to the ground by its four corners. In it were all kinds of four-footed creatures and reptiles and birds of the air. Then he heard a voice saying, "Get up, Peter, kill and eat"' (Acts 10.11–13).

His physical hunger, and the canopy that protected him from the blistering heat of the sun as he prayed in privacy on the roof, might very well have contributed to the graphic content of his vision, with its emphasis on food and a sheet gathered at the four corners. But it certainly didn't detract from the disturbing reality of the message being conveyed, a message Peter was reluctant to accept, and, as it were, came out fighting against. 'By no means, Lord,' he replied to the instruction to kill and eat, 'for I have never eaten anything that is profane or unclean.' But the voice said to him the second time, 'What God has made clean, you must not call profane' (Acts 10.14–15).

The challenge contained in the vision was so important that it was repeated three times. I wonder if, at this point, Peter recalled his threefold denial in the shadow of the cross and his threefold recommissioning in the light of the resurrection? Whatever the reason for it, his initial annoyance was replaced with a sense of uncertainty. 'He was puzzled about what to make of the vision he had seen.' He knew that he had been challenged by something of radical and profound importance, but he wasn't quite sure how he was expected to respond. He felt instinctively that something wider and more fundamental than ceremonial food laws was at stake.

Tumbling barriers

And he was right. He was about to undergo a radical rethink of his religious tradition which would be similar to a conversion experience. At the heart of it would be a stranger called Cornelius, whose messengers were already 'standing by the gate and calling out to ask whether Simon, who was called Peter, was staying there' (Acts 10.17–18). The perplexity that his vision had caused was about to be resolved, and the barriers that divided Jew and Gentile were about to start tumbling down, but it called for obedience and courage on his part.

The messengers had come to invite Peter to the home of Cornelius, a well-known Gentile. They knew that Jews were not permitted to entertain Gentiles in their homes, which is why they stood at the gate and shouted their enquiry about Peter. They also knew that in issuing the invitation they were making life difficult for Peter, for Jews were not permitted by law to enter the home and accept the hospitality of a Gentile. Despite his initial perplexity as to the meaning of his vision, Peter, inspired by the Spirit, knew that the moment for decision had come. 'While Peter was still thinking about the vision, the Spirit said to him, "Look, three men are searching for you. Now get up, go down, and go with them without hesitation; for I have sent them"' (Acts 10.19–20).

He obeyed the Spirit's prompting, met the men and listened to their explanation as to why they had come. He heard that Cornelius had also had a vision, in which an angel had told him to send for Peter and listen to what he had say. It was at that moment, I feel sure, that the penny began to drop. Peter's vision on the roof-top calling upon him to set aside long-standing tradition, and refuse to call profane what God had made clean, clearly referred to this man, Cornelius. The two visions, the three visitors and the prompting of the Spirit indicated to Peter that this was more than a mere coincidence. God, it seemed, was taking the initiative in this, so Peter responded by inviting them in and giving them lodging for the night. He was already beginning to dismantle the barriers of tradition and prejudice.

The next day he took another giant step in that direction when, along with a group of believers from Joppa, he went with the three messengers to the home of Cornelius. There he met a humble host and an expectant household! On his arrival, Cornelius rushed to meet him and knelt at his feet. Embarrassed, Peter quickly put him right. 'Stand up; I am only a mortal' (Acts 10.26). He then went inside, where the whole household had gathered to hear what he had to say. He told them why he had come and they told him why they had sent for him. Together, they recognized the hand of God in the visions each had received.

Cornelius, because of his close association with the Jewish faith, knew that Jewish identity was tied up with a strict observance of food laws and with a separateness from the Gentile nations surrounding them. Only thus could Jews maintain the holiness God required of them (Leviticus 20.24–26; Ezra 10.11). Because of these things, Peter also knew that he was being faced with a challenge to break down a fundamental principle of Jewish community life. But more than that, he was beginning to recognize the full meaning of his roof-top vision.

God had commended Cornelius to him; therefore, he must not consider profane what God had made clean. He must not dismiss nor disregard the approach of Cornelius simply because he was a Gentile. The time had come to set aside Israel's ancient and determined principle of separation. More specifically, the message from God was that the wall or barrier between Jew and Gentile had been removed. He could accept the hospitality of a Gentile household and minister freely to the members of it.

Opening doors

The door was open to proclaim the gospel to the Gentiles. The first privilege to do so fell to Peter, at the invitation of Cornelius, both having been prepared by God for the breakthrough. It was a turning point in the history of the Church. It would never be the same again.

The members of Cornelius' household were the ideal congregation. Their ears, minds and hearts were open, and they were filled with expectation to hear the word of God through Peter. 'All of us are here in the presence of God to listen to all that the Lord has commanded you to say' (Acts 10.33). They were not disappointed.

Peter began to speak, and immediately confirmed the essence of the message that had come from God by vision to Cornelius and him. 'I truly understand that God shows no partiality, but in every nation anyone who fears him and does what is right is acceptable to him' (Acts 10.34). It was a magnificent declaration and must have warmed and lifted the hearts of his hearers. God's good news was for the God-fearing Gentile as well as for the God-fearing Jew. Cornelius and his household had shown themselves ready to receive it, and Peter wasted no time in telling the story to them.

This wonderful story had its focus in Jesus Christ,

the Son of God. He, 'who is Lord of all', was anointed with power and the Spirit. Through his life, death and resurrection, he had revealed 'God's right way of living', and made it possible for all who believe, both Jew and Gentile, to find forgiveness and acceptance with God. The barrier between Jew and Gentile had been broken down. The door which had seemed so firmly closed to Gentiles had been thrown wide open. And what is more, this had been God's plan from the very beginning.

This was indeed good news for the assembled company, and the Spirit set his seal upon it, and upon them, for 'while Peter was still speaking, the Holy Spirit fell upon all who heard the word'. The Jewish believers, who had come from Joppa with Peter, 'were astounded that the gift of the Holy Spirit had been poured out even on the Gentiles, for they heard them speaking in tongues and extolling God' (Acts 10.44–46). It was the story of Pentecost all over again, only this time Gentiles were included.

If, after the two dramatic visions and the Spirit's prompting to go to the home of Cornelius, Peter still had any lingering doubt about embarking on such a departure from tradition, it was completely dispelled by the coming of the Holy Spirit on Cornelius and his household. This Gentile Pentecost marked a significant landmark not only in the life of Cornelius but also in the story of the gospel. As Professor James Dunn has reminded us, 'Cornelius had moved from being acceptable to being accepted and the decisive break-through of God's blessings to the nations had taken place' (Dunn, 1996).

When he had witnessed the power of the Spirit coming upon them, Peter took the next obvious and desirable step by saying, '"Can anyone withhold water for baptizing these people who have received the Holy Spirit as we have?" So he ordered them to be baptized in the name of Jesus Christ' (Acts 10.47–48).

It was a fitting end to a quite remarkable day in the life of Cornelius, but it was not the end of the matter for Peter. During the weeks and months that followed, he had to defend his actions before the Jerusalem church and, indeed, to explain the radical transformation of his attitude to the Gentiles. But he held firm to his convictions and the Jerusalem church ratified the action he had taken. 'When they had heard this, they were silenced. And they praised God, saying, "Then God has given even to the Gentiles the repentance that leads to life"' (Acts 11.17–18).

On the fringe

Cornelius has a unique place in the story of the mission of Jesus Christ. But his experience of being called into partnership with God has been replicated in countless lives across the centuries. Time and time again, God comes to those on the fringe of the church and involves them, often unconsciously, in the work of his kingdom. There are many, like Cornelius, 'upright and God-fearing', who for a variety of reasons are not yet ready to embrace all the traditions and demands of the institutional church. Nevertheless, they are generous and unstinting in their support of the church's work, and prepared to live their lives in the light of Christian values. And God, who shows no partiality, accepts them as they are and works with them and through them to fulfil his purposes of love. The result may not be as boundary-breaking as in the case of Cornelius, but their contribution must not be despised nor dismissed, for in a very real sense they are 'workers together with God'.

12

✍

Tabitha
who sewed for the glory of God

Peggy was a blunt Yorkshire woman with a heart of
gold. Her bluntness, which sometimes bordered on
belligerence, belied a gentle, warm and artistic temperament. She didn't suffer fools gladly, but was
amazingly thoughtful and kind. As a local cleaning
lady, she could not only transform a grubby room but
also bring a sparkle into the life of every family she
helped. She simply couldn't be ignored. Peggy was a
character, a treasure.

But, of all her many talents, her skill with knitting
needles and balls of wool was outstanding. Jumpers,
sweaters, pullovers and cardigans were produced with
the rapidity of a knitting-machine, though the quality
was vastly superior. She didn't knit for profit but for
pleasure. She gave her superb garments as gifts to
other people, tossing them into their unsuspecting
laps and covering her embarrassment by saying, ''Ere
y'are, kid! I'd some spare wool and nowt else to do.'

There was more to Peggy than knitting and cleaning, however. She had a wonderful eye for colour and

design and an unerring sensitivity towards those in need. At a time of grave personal illness, I was on the receiving end of that sensitivity and care. Invariably, she left me feeling better than she found me. When she herself became ill and died, many mourned the loss of a dear friend, and since the church service was held on a cold November morning several of them were wearing Peggy's woollen pullovers! It is almost impossible for me to read the story of Tabitha without recalling with gratitude the life and talents of my friend, Peggy.

Condensed history

I have told Peggy's story, known only to her friends, in just three hundred words. Tabitha's story is summed up in far less – only seven verses, during which she lives, dies and lives again (Acts 9.36–42). Her story, however, is known worldwide and has been a continuing source of inspiration and encouragement to millions throughout the centuries – and with good reason.

Like Peggy, she was quite a character. Her reputation within the local community was high, especially among the widows, for she was a dab hand with a needle and thread. Indeed, her discipleship as a follower of Jesus Christ was expressed not just in prayer but in practical down-to-earth Christianity.

But we might never have known of the abiding characteristic of her life if she had not fallen ill and died. It seems to be one of the great ironies of life that it is often only after death that the significance of our time on earth becomes apparent and we are truly appreciated.

That was certainly true of Tabitha. Her name is the Aramaic word for a gazelle. Dorcas, the other name by which she was known, is the Greek for the same word. She lived up to her name not only by the speed with which she appears and disappears from the Bible story, but also in the gracefulness and beauty of her life. Her death caused great consternation throughout her local community, not just among her Christian friends. So much so that they decided to do something dramatic about it.

If Tabitha had died in Jerusalem, she would have been buried the same day, for that was the law. I guess that also would have been the end of the matter. Outside Jerusalem, however, burial had to take place within three days. So, dying in Joppa (modern Jaffa, which is linked to the new Jewish city of Tel-Aviv), her friends observed local custom and washed her and laid her out in an upstairs room. Then they completely broke with custom and sent for Peter. It seemed that they were not prepared to let death take their friend Dorcas without doing something about it, such was the impact she had had upon them during her life.

Good news travels fast, and they had heard that Peter was in the nearby town of Lydda and had just cured a man who for years had been bedridden with paralysis. It was almost too good to be true. It brought a sense of both hope and urgency into the situation, and 'the disciples, who heard that Peter was there, sent two men to him with the request, "Please come to us without delay"' (Acts 9.39).

Tangible discipleship

Peter, always a man of action, couldn't refuse such an urgent request. He made the short journey to the home of Tabitha, and was immediately taken to the upstairs room, where he saw not only her lifeless body, but also clear and tangible evidence of the essence of her discipleship. She, although dead, yet spoke, through the presence and tears of the widows who had gathered, and the garments they wore. Here was visible testimony to the gracefulness and usefulness of Tabitha and why, instinctively, they had sent for Peter.

Tabitha had been introduced to the story as 'a disciple who was devoted to good works and acts of charity'. Whether or not she had ever met James, she certainly was completely in tune with his fundamental message that 'faith by itself, if it has no works, is dead' (James 2.17). She was also motivated by the Jewish emphasis on charitable works towards the needy, especially the widows. Her love for the needy sprang out of her love for God. Her faith found expression in practical acts of kindness. Others had been given gifts of prophecy or preaching, evangelism or teaching. Tabitha had been given the gift of sewing. A needle and thread, allied to a righteous life, kind heart and generous spirit, were the means whereby she brought glory to God.

Indeed, by her almsgiving and charity towards the widows she was revealing an aspect of the character of God, who has a special concern for orphans and widows and views those who care for them as righteous, doing that which is right in his eyes. 'Religion that is pure and undefiled before God the Father, is this: to care for orphans and widows in their distress, and to keep oneself unstained by the world' (James 1.27).

Peter had probably never met Tabitha before. When he met the widows of the Christian community in Joppa, however, they soon put him in the picture regarding the outstanding quality of her life and service. It was a most moving testimony, though they don't appear to have used many words. Instead, they used visual aids, pointing to the clothes they were wearing. 'All the widows stood beside him, weeping and showing tunics and other clothing that Dorcas had made during her time with them' (Acts 9.39). It was a fashion display with a difference, and it spoke volumes about Tabitha's ministry of generosity and the gratitude of the widows within her community.

Their tearful message wouldn't have been lost on Peter, but he had work to do and wanted to get on with it, so he put them all out of the room. He wasn't being dismissive of the widows; on the contrary, he was responding to the grief and the gratitude they had been expressing regarding Tabitha. So, as soon as the door of the upstairs room had closed behind the weeping widows, Peter began the first of three stages of an amazing ministry.

Life goes on

He got his priorities right. The first thing he did was pray. It was a clear acknowledgement that the powerful help needed in such circumstances was to be found in God. Then turning, as it were, from heaven to earth, he spoke gently but with authority to the body that had been laid out with such love and devotion, 'Tabitha, get up.' And she did! 'She opened her eyes and, seeing Peter, she sat up.' Then, just as Jesus had done with the daughter of Jairus, Peter 'gave her his hand and helped her up'. He then moved to the third and final stage of his ministry in that upper room, for having spoken to God and to the body of Tabitha, he now called the believers, including the widows, who were in the house, to come back into the room to see that Tabitha was alive.

It was a dramatic transformation and one which had been based on a well-tried methodology. Peter's actions had some similarities to those of Elijah and Elisha (1 Kings 17.17–24 and 2 Kings 4.32–37) and, as noted above, it was almost a mirror image of the actions of Jesus in the restoration to life of Jairus' daughter (Mark 5.35–43). Some New Testament scholars and commentators are of the opinion that these similarities could seem a little contrived and that Luke, the author of Acts, may have had a particular reason for shaping the story in the way he did. What seems beyond question, however, is that the understanding of those who were present, including the widows who wept, and the wider community in Joppa who mourned, was that Tabitha had been raised from the dead.

The personal story of Tabitha or Dorcas seems to end rather abruptly. The tears of grief from the widows at her death was plain for all to see, but no mention is made of their reaction at seeing her alive again. We are left guessing as to the subsequent shape and direction of her new lease of life. Was her needle and thread busier than ever? Did her commitment to good works and acts of charity intensify?

Luke does not tell us. Instead, he allows us to assume that Tabitha's practical discipleship went on as before, because he wants to put her life of compassionate service into a larger context. And so, following the experience of being raised from death, her recorded story ends with these words: 'This became known throughout Joppa, and many believed in the Lord.' The fact that Tabitha lived, died and lived again became a means whereby the gospel and the number of believers increased. It is not without significance that her story marks the prelude to a major outward movement of the Church in mission. After he had raised Tabitha to new life, Peter stayed in Joppa for some time with Simon, a tanner. It was to be a period of preparation for involvement in one of the great turning points in the life and history of the Church of Jesus Christ, as the gospel was preached and the door of acceptance was opened to the Gentiles.

By the grace of God, great things were achieved by spiritual giants like Peter and Paul. They helped to shape the history of the Church and, through their written words, continue to inspire people and communities of faith throughout the world. By comparison, Tabitha is not worth mentioning, some would say – but not God. His story of the early Church and the spread of the gospel would be incomplete without Tabitha and her needle and thread.

Epilogue

'People are the words with which God tells his story.'

So wrote Edward Schillebeeckx, the Dutch professor of theology, in his scholarly book, *Church: The Human Story of God*. He was quoting the words of a young boy, and used them as the opening sentence of the foreword to his book because they served to introduce his readers to its theme.

Not Least in the Kingdom does not pretend to be a scholarly book, but it has been written with the conviction that the wisdom of that young boy was profound. God tells his story through human beings. And not only through the great and the gifted, but also through the weak, the vulnerable and the unknown.

One of the many joys of retirement is being allowed to descend from the episcopal pedestal, where some have tried to maroon me over the years, and to live in an ordinary house, in an ordinary street and enjoy the company of ordinary neighbours. The joy has come through the discovery of so many people who, quietly and without fuss, are making a significant contribution to the life of their local community or their local church.

They blow no trumpets, they desire no reward, they find their satisfaction and fulfilment in the sacrificial service they give to others. And, like those in the parable of the Last Judgement, they are surprised and embarrassed if attention is drawn to the value of what they are doing.

> 'Lord, when was it that we saw you hungry and gave you food, or thirsty and gave you something to drink? And when was it that we saw you a stranger and welcomed you, or naked and gave you clothing? And when was it that we saw you sick or in prison and visited you?' And the king will answer them, 'Truly I tell you, just as you did it to one of the least of these who are members of my family, you did it to me.'
>
> (Matthew 25.37–40)

Jesus taught that though such people may be out of sight, they are not out of mind. They may seem to be nonentities in an aggressive, selfish and competitive society, but in the eyes of God they are inheritors of the kingdom of heaven.

References

Alison, James, *Knowing Jesus*. SPCK, 1993, 2nd edn 1998.

Blanch, Stuart Y., *Encounters with Jesus*. Hodder & Stoughton, 1988.

Brown, Raymond E., *The Gospel According to John*. Geoffrey Chapman, 1971.

Browning, Robert, 'Prospice', in *A Poem a Day*, ed. Karen McCosker and Nicholas Albery. Steerforth Press, 1996.

Dunn, J. G., *Acts of the Apostles*. Epworth Press, 1996.

The Writings of Irenaeus, vol. 1. T. & T. Clark, 1886.

Schillebeeckx, Edward, *Church: The Human Story of God*. SCM Press, 1990.

Taylor, John V., *The Go-Between God*. SCM Press, 1972.